Copyright © 2019 Vicki Sassoon

ALL RIGHTS RESERVED. This book contains material protected under International and Federal Copyright Laws and Treaties. Any unauthorized reprint or use of this material is prohibited.

No part of this book may be reproduced or transmitted in any form or by any means, electronic or mechanical , including photocopying, recording, or by any information storage and retrieval system without express written permission of the author.

Printed in the United States

First Printing 2019

Contents

INTRODUCTION

7	About the Author
9	Background

SALADS

12	Arugula Salad		40	Chickpeas with Beets Salad
14	Swiss Chard Salad with Strawberry Dressing		42	Collard Green Salad with Fruit
18	Baby Kale Salad with Raspberry Dressing		44	Steamed Green Bean & Pine Nuts Salad
20	Black Eye Peas Salad		46	Quinoa and Black Bean Salad
22	Boston Lettuce Salad		48	Red Cabbage Salad
24	Butternut Squash and Black Beans Salad		50	Tabbouleh Salad with Quinoa
26	Kale Salad		52	Broccoli with Flax Seed Dressing
28	Fresh Green Beans with Kale Salad		54	Zucchini Ravioli
30	Cucumber Salad		56	Steamed Cauliflower with Basil Dressing
32	Spinach Salad		58	Lettuce & Pear Salad with Basil Dressing
34	Tofu Salad with Collard Green		60	Savoy Cabbage Salad
36	Millet with Pinto Beans Salad		62	Kohlrabi & Cucumber Salad
38	Fresh Herbs Dressing			

SOUPS

68	Black Eye Peas Soup		78	Lentil and Swiss Chard Soup
70	Butternut Squash Soup		80	Split Peas Soup
72	Great Northern Bean Soup		82	Green Beans Soup
76	Spinach Soup with Pinto Beans or Chickpeas			

Contents

STEWS & RICE DISHES

86	Okra Stew	104	Lemon Zucchini with Herbs (Nana'iyi)
88	Dolmma Stew	108	Curry Okra Stew
92	Eggplant Stew *(Tepsi)*	112	Green Rice
96	Biryani Veggie Mix	116	Yellow Rice
98	Cauliflower Tepsi	118	Kitchree Rice (Lentil Rice)

VEGETARIAN BURGERS, DIPS & SPREADS

122	Black Beans & Kale Burger	132	Cauliflower Patties
124	Brown Rice Veggie-Burger	136	Hummus with Herbs Dip
126	Chickpeas Dip or Burger	138	Chickpeas Sambousak Spread
128	Quinoa with Fresh Herbs & Raw Nuts	140	Cooking Dry Chickpeas

FERMENTED PICKLES

144	Fermented Turnip Pickles - *Im'Chalela*	152	Fermented Red Cabbage
146	Fermented Sweet Potato / Yam	156	Fermented Chinese Cabbage
148	Fermented Savoy Cabbage *(Sauerkraut)*	160	Cucumber Pickles

FOR A SWEET TOOTH!

164	Date Sweets *(Medgoga)*

About the Author

Vicki Sassoon is a caring and compassionate woman. Originally from Iraq, Vicki spent her early life graduating with a degree in physics with the goal of becoming a teacher. Vicki achieved this goal, becoming a lab demonstrator at the University of Baghdad lab for two years. After she and her family fled to London, Vicki got married and came to New York with her husband where she raised her family. Vicki is a very family-oriented person who now dedicates all her energy to caring to all those around her; caring for her husband, son, family, and community in every way that she is capable of.

Vicki is especially devoted to helping those in need by passing all that she has learned through herself about health onto those around her.

Vicki is a home cook who is passionate about making food that is just as healthy as it is delicious. As a home cook with a middle eastern background, Vicki enjoys food and cooking very much and draws on influences from her mother's traditional recipes. However, with a growing desire to maintain a healthy lifestyle, Vicki adapted her cooking style to include healthy and raw ingredients without compromising on the tastes she loves.

When cooking, Vicki does her best to use the ingredients at hand, and relies on her smell and taste to create the dishes that she and her family love. In this collection of recipes, Vicki has undertaken the task of measuring the ingredients she uses and breaking down each step so that you the reader can recreate these delicious and healthy recipes. While she also has many recipes that include gluten and meat, she chose not to include them in this book keeping it healthy and tasty for all different kinds of people.

Background

Dear Reader

Within the pages of this book, you will find a cornucopia of vegan delights. The recipes combine the tastes of my Middle Eastern background and passion for cooking nutritious everyday meals of; Salads, Soups, Vegetarian Patties, Dips, Fermented foods, Stews and Rice Dishes.

The dishes amalgamate raw foods and cooked cuisine, using spices and fresh herbs inspired from the Middle East. The Recipes in this book;

◊ Offers nothing fried thereby conserving the goodness of the ingredients

◊ Includes a variety of beans and non-gluten grains for their taste and protein value

◊ Ensures ingredients are vegan, gluten free, dairy free and sugar free

When my husband was diagnosed with Cancer, over nine years ago, he refused to go through chemo or radiation therapy and wanted to maintain a vegan healthy and nutrition rich diet for his path back to health.

My background meant that I loved to cook vegetarian and meaty dishes alike. So when my husband decided to fight his cancer through a vegan diet, I had to switch my cooking to be fully vegan but yet provide all the nutrients required as part of a healthy and balanced diet.

I also wanted to cook food which had all the tongue tingling tastes of the Mediterranean, which we were all used to. I would tell friends and family what I was doing and as time went on and the dishes became varied and popular, they all began to ask for the recipes. The result of my efforts are the collection of recipes you will find within this book.

Note: All cooked dishes in this book have been prepared with gas range unit. If you are using electric range, then I recommend the use of two burners, one for medium and other for low to switch the pot, as it takes time for electric burners to switch from medium to low. Also note that cooking time may vary for eclectic burners as the temperature may be different. If you are using electric ovens the cooking time for baking and grilling may also slightly vary.

Enjoy!
Vicki Sassoon

Copyright ©Vicki Sassoon 2019

Salads

Arugula Salad

Serves: 2 to 3

Prep Time: 20 min
Cook Time: N/A

Preparations

1:
Trim the ends of the Arugula, then pile leaves and finely chop. Cut the fennel in half, and remove the large stems, setting aside the fine leaves. Place the flat side of the bulb down, then thinly slice and dice. (picture 1)

2:
Remove thick stems from cilantro, piling the rest and chopping finely.

3:
In a large bowl, mix all the ingredients (apart from the crushed almonds) together.

4:
Sprinkle the crushed almonds on top.

Note: You can keep this in the fridge for up to 2 days.

Ingredients

Arugula
2 bunches of Arugula, about 4 cups chopped in small pieces (with stems)

Avocado
1 Avocado, 3/4 of a cup cut in small pieces

Zucchini
1 small Zucchini, 3/4 of a cup cut in small pieces, with skin if organic

Cilantro (Coriander)
1 bunch of fresh Cilantro, 3/4 of a cup finely chopped

Fennel
1 small head bunch of fresh fennel, 3/4 of a cup finely chopped (fine green leaves can be used, but remove the stems)

Almond Oil
3 tablespoons of almond oil

Himalayan Pink Salt
A pinch of Himalayan Pink Salt, about 1/8 teaspoon

Lemon Juice
3-4 tablespoons of freshly squeezed lemon juice

Raw Almonds
2 tablespoons of coarsely crushed raw almonds (using knife or food processor)

Salads

Steps...

1. Trim the ends of the stems, pile the leaves, then finely chop as shown

2. Dice up the courgettes

3. Remove thick roots by knife, then finely chop the fennel. Fine green leaves can be used, but remove the stems

Cut in half

Discard stems

Save and include small greens

Slice and dice

4. Cut avocadoes

5. Pile and chop up the cilantro (including thin stems) and crush the Almonds

6. Sprinkle crushed almonds on top, and serve

Salads

Swiss Chard Salad with Strawberry Dressing

Serves: 2 to 3

Prep Time: 25 min
Cook Time: N/A

Preparations

1:
Remove and discard the stems of the Swiss Chard, piling the leaves, then chopping into strips, then again into small pieces. (Picture 1)

2:
Cut the fennel in half, and remove the large stems, setting aside the fine leaves. Place the flat side of the bulb down, then thinly slice and dice.

3:
Cut the zucchini (with skin if it is organic) and the avocado into small pieces. Clean the basil and chop. (Picture 3)

4:
Place all the dressing ingredients in a blender and blend very well until very smooth. Then add some fresh crushed nuts on top. (picture 4)

5:
In a bowl mix the Swiss Chard, Fennel, Zucchini, Avocado, Tarragon, Basil, Pine nuts and crushed pumpkin seeds. (picture 5)

6:
Pour dressing on top of the salad and mix together. (picture 5)

NOTES
- Make the dressing just before serving for best taste and freshness. Use dressing within the same day.
- You can use Boston Lettuce instead of Swiss Chard

Ingredients

The Salad

Swiss Chard
3 Cups chopped without stem Swiss Chard

Fennel
1-2 Cups chopped in small pieces Fennel

Zucchini
1 cup chopped in small pieces Zucchini

Avocado
1 large avocado cut in small pieces

Basil
1 cup chopped fresh Basil

Raw Pumpkin Seeds
2 tablespoons coarsely crushed pumpkin seeds

Raw Pine Nuts
2 tablespoons Pine Nuts

Tarragon
1/4 teaspoon dry Tarragon or 2 tablespoons of finely chopped fresh Tarragon

Fresh Sage *(Optional)*
1 tablespoon

The Dressing

Frozen Organic Strawberries
1/4 cup small frozen strawberries (about 4-5 medium strawberries)

Fresh Pineapple
Cut into small pieces, about 1/2 cup.

Garlic
2 cloves of garlic (about 1 tablespoon crushed)

Mustard powder
1/2 teaspoon mustard powder

Almond oil
1 tablespoon Almond oil

Himalayan Pink Salt
A pinch (about 1/8 teaspoon) Himalayan Pink Salt

Salads

Steps... 1/3

1. Remove the stems of the swiss chard, pile the leaves, roll, and cut into strips

2. Remove thick roots with knife, then Finely chop the Fennel. (Fine green leaves can be used, but remove the stems)

Cut in Half

Slice and dice

Discard stems
Save and include small greens

Steps... 2/3

3. Chop the zucchini and avocado as shown. Clean basil and chop

4. Crush the nuts and prepare the dressing

Salads

Steps... 3/3

5. Mix salad with dressing and serve (left to right)

Chopped vegetables and herbs

Shown with dressing

Fresh basil leaves on top.

Salad shown with Swiss Chard: Ready to serve.

Optional: You can use Boston Lettuce instead of Swiss Chard

Baby Kale Salad with Raspberry Dressing

Serves: 2 to 3

Prep Time: 25 min
Cook Time: N/A

Preparations

1:
To prepare the dressing, place the raspberries, oil, salt and lime juice in a blender until very smooth, then transfer into a small bowl and add the crushed pumpkin seeds, hempseeds, grated apple and the chopped celery leaves and mix together.

2:
To prepare the salad, mix all the chopped vegetables (Baby Kale, celery, red apple, avocado & red onion) in a large bowl then add the raspberry dressing on top and mix well before serving.

Ingredients

The Salad

Baby Kale
5 Cups chopped Baby Kale

Celery
2 Cups chopped Celery

Red Apple
1 small red Apple cubed

Avocado
1 medium Avocado cubed

Red Onion
1 small red Onion finely chopped

The Dressing

Frozen Raspberries
1/2 cup frozen raspberries

Raw Pumpkin Seeds
2 tablespoons crushed pumpkin seeds

Celery Leaves
2 tablespoons Celery leaves finely chopped

Red Apple
1/4 red grated Apple

Hemp Seeds
3 tablespoons raw hulled hemp seeds

Hemp Seed Oil (or Olive Oil)
3 tablespoons hemp seed oil

Fresh Lime
1 fresh lime juiced

Himalayan Pink Salt
1/4 teaspoon Himalayan Pink Salt

Salads

Steps...

1. Prepare ingredients for dressing. Grate the apple and chop the celery leaves. Crush the pumpkin seeds with a coffee grinder or small food processor.

2. Dressing ready to mix with salad.

3. Prepare ingredients for Salad

4. Mix salad with dressing and serve.

Salads

Black Eye Peas Salad

Serves: 2

Prep Time: 20 min
Cook Time: 30 min *(for*

Preparations

1:
Soak one cup of dry Black Eye Peas overnight (8 hours), drain and place in a pot adding 5 cups of water and bring to the boil. Scoop out most of the foam (quickly for about a minute) that is formed while bringing to the boil. Then simmer for 20-30 minutes ensuring the Peas don't go mushy and stay whole. Drain the Peas and let it cool down.

2:
Crush 1 tablespoon of flax seeds (either manually or in a food processor).

Note: Try to grind the flax seeds yourself. It will taste nicer and more nutritious than when brought ready-ground.

3:
Add the Lemon juice, chopped Parsley, chopped Mint, chopped spring Onions, crushed flax seeds, and the olive oil to the cooled down Peas with a pinch of salt and mix. Ready to serve.

Note: This can keep in the refrigerator for up to 4 days and should always be served cold (never heat).

Serve with optional sliced cherry tomatoes on top.

Ingredients

Black Eye Peas
1 cup dry Black Eye Peas, 2 cups cooked

Lemon
4 Tablespoons fresh lemon Juice

Fresh Parsley
4 tablespoons finely chopped fresh Parsley

Fresh Mint
4 tablespoon finely chopped fresh Mint leaves, or 1 tablespoon dry

Flax Seeds
1 tablespoon Flax Seeds

Spring Onion—Scallions
2 tablespoons finely chopped scallions

Olive Oil
2 tablespoons olive oil

Himalayan Pink Salt
1 Pinch of Himalayan Pink Salt, about 1/8 teaspoon

Salads

Steps...

1. Flax Seeds Crushed

3. Pile the parsley into a small the thick part of the stems

5. Serve with optional sliced

and finely chop the Mint leaves

nds of the scallions, cut in half,

Salads

Boston Lettuce Salad

Serves: 2 – 3

Prep Time: 20 min
Cook Time: N/A

Preparations

1:
Thoroughly wash and dry all vegetables before chopping.

2:
Pile the lettuce leaves and chop them.

Note: You can use other kinds of lettuce instead of Boston, Romain, Green, Red Leaf Lettuce

3:
Pile the Parsley in small bunch in your hand removing the thick part of the stems, then finely chop.

4:
Finely chop the cilantro and dill in the same way that you chopped the parsley.

5:
Slice then chop the tomato into small pieces. Peel the onion, cut in half, then with the flat side down slice length wise then turn and cut into small pieces.

6:
Combine all the ingredients in a large bowl adding the salt, lemon juice, crushed walnuts and walnut oil. Mix well before serving.

Ingredients

Boston Lettuce (1 medium head)
5 cups chopped Boston lettuce

Cilantro (coriander)
1 cup finely chopped Cilantro

Parsley
1 and 1/2 cup finely chopped Parsley

Dill
1 and 1/2 cup finely chopped Dill

Cucumber
1 cup cubed cucumber

Tomato
1 cup Tomatoes cut in small pieces

Red Onion
1/2 chopped Red Onion

Raw Walnuts
2 Tablespoons coarsely crushed Walnuts, with a knife or food processor

Lemon
1 fresh lemon juiced, about 4 tablespoons

Walnut oil (or Olive oil)
2 tablespoons Walnut oil

Himalayan Pink Salt
A pinch of Himalayan Pink Salt, about 1/4 teaspoon Himalayan Pink Salt

Salads

Steps...

1. Wash before chopping

2. Remove the thick part of the Parsley and Dill. Pile and chop.

3. Chop, then combine all ingredients as shown

Cilantro

Parsley

Dill

Lettuce

Cucumber

Tomato

Onion

Salads

Butternut Squash and Black Beans Salad

Serves: 2 – 3

Prep Time: 15 min
Cook Time: 40 min

Preparations

1: To prepare the Black Beans, soak overnight, drain and place in a pot. Cover the Beans with water (about 2 inches on top) and bring to rapid boil, quickly scooping most of the foam that is formed for about a minute. Lower the heat and simmer for about 30-40 minutes. Then drain the Beans and let it cool down to use for the salad. Check the beans halfway through the cooking to make sure that they are not overcooked, you do not want it mushy, just tender.

2: To prepare the Butternut Squash, peel, remove the seeds, then cut into large pieces. Steam for about 13-15 minutes, test with a fork, it should be tender but not too soft. Let it cool down in a plate then cut into small pieces.

3: Cut the Avocado in half, remove the pit, slice in cubes inside the peel, then scoop out with a spoon. Crush the Pine Nuts and Pumpkin Seeds with a knife. *(see pic 2)*

4: Combine all the ingredients in a bowl (Making sure the beans and the butternut squash are fully cooled down) and mix well before serving. The salad can keep in the fridge for up to 3 days, eaten cold, never heat.

Note: You can prepare the Black Beans and leave in the fridge and use within three days.

Ingredients

Butternut Squash
1/2 a Butternut Squash cut in 4 inch length pieces *(see pic 1)*

Black Beans
1/2 cup dry Black Beans—soaked overnight in water, which makes 1 cup cooked.

Parsley
1 cup chopped Parsley

Avocado
1 Avocado, cut in small cubes, about one cup

Red Onion
1/2 cup red Onion diced

Pine Nuts
1 tablespoon crushed Pine Nuts

Raw Pumpkin Seeds
1 tablespoon crushed Pumpkin seeds

Lemon
The juice of fresh lemon (1/4 cup, about 3 tablespoons)

Olive Oil
2 tablespoons Olive oil

Himalayan Pink Salt
A pinch of Himalayans pink salt, about 1/8—1/4 teaspoon

Salads

Steps...

1. Prepare all ingredients. Sliced Butternut Squash and cooked black Beans

2. Crush the Pine Nuts and Pumpkin Seeds with a knife

Steam then cut Butternut squash

Salads

Kale Salad

Serves: 2

Prep Time: 15 min
Stand Time: 180 min

Ingredients

Kale *(any kind)*
5 cups chopped Kale (without the stem)

Celery
1-2 cups celery chopped in small pieces

Raw Hemp Seed
3 tablespoons raw hulled hemp seeds

Hemp Seed Oil
2 tablespoons hemp seed oil

Lime
1 fresh lime - juiced

Himalayan Pink Salt
1/4 teaspoon Himalayan Pink Salt

Preparations

1:
Remove the stem from the Kale, pile and hold the leaves together, then finely chop (see pic 2)

2:
Cut the celery into strips lengthways then hold them together in a bunch and chop into very small pieces (see pic 3)

3:
Mix the Kale and the celery in a bowl and add the hemp seeds, hemp seed oil, lime juice and salt mixing them all together

4:
Allow to stand for a few hours to soften and enhance the taste of the hemp seeds before serving or alternatively you can leave to stand overnight.

Steps...

1. Prepare ingredients.

2. Remove and discard the stems from the Kale and chop leaves as shown.

3. Peel and cut the Celery lengthways *(left)*, then hold together and chop into small pieces *(right)*.

Fresh Green Beans with Kale Salad

Serves: 2—3

Prep Time: 15 min
Stand Time: 60 min

Preparations

1: Line the green beans and cut them in small pieces about 1/4 inch.

2: Remove stem from Kale and roll the leaves if flat or hold together if curly, and chop them small *(pic 2)*.

3: Peel and cut the celery in strips then hold together and cut small.

4: Crush the Pecans with a knife or crush coarse with a food processor. *(pic 4)*

5: Use half green apple and half red apple, keep the skin on (if organic) and cut into small cubes. *(pic 5)*

6: Cut the mango into cubes, same size as the apple cubes. *(pic 5)*

7: Peel and cut the onion in half, face the flat side on the cutting board, cut in strips, then dice into small tiny pieces. *(pic 5)*

8: Finely chop the Parsley and the Mint.

9: Cut the Avocado in half, remove the pit, slice in cubes inside the peel then scoop it out with a spoon. *(pic 5)*

10: Mix all the ingredients in a large bowl, adding oil, salt, lemon juice and cranberry on top. Leave to stand for an hour while all the flavors soak up before serving. *(Pic 6)*

Ingredients

Green Beans
1 cup fresh green Beans chopped into small pieces (about 1/2 inch each piece)

Red Kale
4 cups red Kale thinly chopped (without stem)

Celery
1 cup Celery, cut into small pieces (about 1/2 inch in each piece)

Spring or Red Onions
3-4 tablespoons spring or red Onions diced very small

Red Apple
1/2 red Apple cut in small cubes

Green Apple
1/2 green Apple cut in small cubes

Mango
1 medium fresh Mango (about 3/4 cup chopped in small pieces, half an inch each piece)

Avocado
1 medium Avocado cubed

Dried Cranberry *(Optional)*
2 tablespoons dried cranberry

Fresh Parsley
1 tablespoon finely chopped Parsley

Fresh Mint
1 tablespoon finely chopped mint

Raw Pecans
1/2 cup of crushed raw pecans

Hempseeds
2 tablespoons hulled Hempseeds

Fresh Lemon
Fresh Lemon juice (1/4 cup, about 3 tablespoons)

Olive oil or Hempseed oil
3 tablespoons olive oil or Hempseed oil

Salads

Steps...

1. Prepare ingredients.

2. Remove the stem from the Kale and roll the leaves and chop them small.

3. Peel and cut the Celery lengthways *(left)*, then hold together and chop into small pieces *(right)*.

4. Crush the Pecans with a knife or crush coarse with a food processor.

5. All ingredients cut and ready to mix.

6. Mix all the ingredients in a large bowl, adding a pinch of salt to taste. Leave to stand for an hour while all the flavours soak up before serving.

If using spring onions finely chop as shown.

Salads

Cucumber Salad

Serves: 2—3

Prep Time: 15 min
Cook Time: N/A

Preparations

1:
Chop the cucumber in small pieces *(pic 2)*.

2:
Cut the Avocado in half, remove the pit, slice in cubes inside the peel then scoop it out with a spoon.

3:
Cut the tomato and onion.

4:
Clean the fresh herbs, remove all the stems from the Basil, Parsley, Thyme & Mint and chop very finely. (Do not use dry herbs for this recipe, only fresh).

5:
Add the chopped herbs to the rest of the ingredients in the bowl.

6:
Add the Olive Oil, Lemon juice, hemp seeds and salt. Mix thoroughly before serving.

Hint: Make sure you chop all the vegetables with a knife and not a food processor to preserve the texture of the vegetables.

Ingredients

English Cucumber
1 large English Cucumber chopped in small cubes *(about 1/2 inch)* measuring about 4 cups

Tomato
1 small tomato chopped very small *(about 1/4 inch)* measuring about 1 cup

Avocado
1 small Avocado cut into small cubes *(about 1/2 inch)*

Fresh Basil, Parsley, Thyme & Mint
1 cup combined of finely chopped fresh herbs: Basil, Parsley, Thyme and Mint

Raw Hemp Seeds
2 tablespoons raw hulled Hemp seeds

Red Onion
1 small finely chopped red Onion, measuring about 1/2 cup

Olive Oil
1 - 2 tablespoons Olive Oil

Lemon
2 tablespoons fresh lemon juice *(or to your taste)*

Himalayan Pink Salt
1/4 teaspoon Himalayan Pink Salt *(or to your taste)*

Salads

Steps...

1. Fresh herbs: (left to right) Basil, Parsley, Thyme & Mint

Other optional fresh herbs included here e.g. rosemary and lemon balm herbs.

2. Chop small each of the ingredients as shown.

Salads

Spinach Salad

Serves: 3

Prep Time: 20-25 min
Cook Time: N/A

Preparations

1:
Clean the Spinach, Parsley, Coriander and Dill as shown in the steps pictures.

2:
Peel and cut the onion in half, face the flat side on the cutting board, cut in strips, then in small tiny pieces diced.

3:
Add the cooked Pinto or Kidney Beans, refer to the cooking method in the dry chickpeas recipe in this book. *(Or you can use cooked Pinto Beans or Red Kidney Beans; both can be cooked in the same method as the dry chickpeas).*

4:
Mix everything and add fresh lemon juice, salt and olive oil to taste.

This can be kept in the fridge for up to 2 days.

Ingredients

Spinach
4 cups fresh Spinach chopped with the stem or use baby spinach

Parsley
1 cup fresh Parsley chopped

Coriander (Cilantro)
1 cup fresh Coriander chopped with the thin stem

Dill
1 cup fresh Dill chopped with the thin stem

Red Onion
1 small red onion (about 1/2 cup chopped)

Chickpeas or Pinto Beans
1 cup of cooked Chickpeas or Pinto Beans

Olive Oil
2 tablespoons Olive Oil / or add amount to your own taste

Lemon
2 tablespoons fresh lemon juice / or add amount to your own taste

Himalayan Pink Salt
1/4 teaspoon Himalayan Pink Salt

Steps...

1. Prepare and chop the Spinach. Remove the large bottom of the root (first left pic), then pile and coarsely chop the rest as shown (second and third pic). Or you can use chopped baby spinach (fourth right pic).

2. Cut and discard the thick part of the Parsley, pile the rest with its own thin stems and chop (right pic).

3. Pile the dill (left pic) and chop with its own stem (right pic).

4. Pile and chop the Coriander (Cilantro) with its own thin stems, in the same way as the Parsley, as shown.

5. Mix everything and add fresh lemon juice, salt and olive oil to taste.

Ready to serve.

Tofu Salad with Collard Green

Serves: 3-4

Prep Time: 25 min
Cook Time: N/A

Preparations

1:
Remove the stems from the Collard green, pile the leaves, roll them together then slice them thinly and cut them across once at the end. Open them up with your hands, they should be long thin strings. *(pic 3)*

2:
Use the very inside of the Celery heart, it is very soft. Or use just the Celery leaves and chop them finely.

3:
Crush the nuts with the food processor separately.

4:
Crush the flax seeds with a food processor or a grinder. Fresh crushed flax seeds always tastes nicer than the ready crushed ones.

5:
Mix all the ingredients together then top it with extra Pecans cut in small pieces before serving.

6:
You can serve right away, or leave in fridge for a few hours or overnight, allowing all the flavors to absorb together.

Ingredients

Tofu
Organic extra firm Tofu (7 ounce, which is about 1 and 1/2 cups diced)

Collard Green
3 medium leaves which is about 2 cups finely chopped

Celery heart or leaves
1 cup finely chopped Celery hearts or leaves

Raw Macadamia
2 tablespoons crushed of Macadamia or Pecans

Raw Almonds or Raw Pecan Nuts
2 tablespoons crushed Almonds or Pecans

Lemon
2-3 tablespoons of fresh lemon juice

Dry Cranberry
1 tablespoon dry cranberry

Raw Flax seeds
1 teaspoon of crushed flax seeds

Green Italian Olives
1 to 2 large green Italian Olives chopped into small pieces

Olive or Flax seed oil
1 tablespoons Olive Oil or flax seed oil

Himalayan Pink Salt
1/8 teaspoon Himalayan Pink Salt

Salads

Steps...

1. List of ingredients.

2. Slice and cut the Tofu in small pieces.

3. Remove and discard the stem, pile together, then roll up the leaves and slice thin, then open them up as shown below. The way you cut makes a difference to the taste and texture of the Salad.

4. Crushed Macadamia Nuts.

5. Crushed Flax Seeds

Salads

Millet with Pinto Beans Salad

Serves: 3-4

Prep Time: 20 min
Cook Time: 30-40 min

Ingredients

Millet
1 cup Millet (not cooked)

Dill
1/2 to 3/4 cup chopped Dill

Onion
1 small Onion about 1/2 cup finely chopped Onion

Pinto Beans
1 cup dry Pinto Beans, which makes 2 cups cooked

Olive Oil
1 tablespoon Olive Oil

Himalayan Pink Salt
A pinch of Himalayan pink salt about 1/8 teaspoon Olive Oil

Preparations

1:
Soak one cup of Pinto beans for 8 hours or overnight . Drain the Pinto Beans and place in a pot, add 4 cups of water and bring to rapid boil uncovered. Then quickly remove most of the white foam that is formed while boiling for a minute (see pic 3). Add one teaspoon of salt, cover and simmer on low heat for about an hour. Leave the lid on throughout the simmering to allow the beans to cook thoroughly *(don't open the lid too often to allow the beans to cook)*. Once cooked, drain and leave to stand.

2:
To prepare the Dill, pile all the dill into a bunch (see pic 1), remove the large part of the stem but leave the thin part of the stem and then chop up finely.

3:
Finely Chop up the Onion. (pic 2)

4:
In a medium size pot, add the Pinto Beans, Millet, salt, olive oil, chopped Dill, Onions and about 2 cups of water *(ensure the ingredients are covered by half an inch of water not more)*, mix and bring to the boil while uncovered. Stirring a few times, cover and simmer on low heat for 30-40 minutes. It should be ready when all the water is absorbed. Serve while hot.

Note: You can keep up to 5 days in the fridge. To reheat, place the pot on low heat until steams again. Or you may serve this cold with fresh chopped parsley sprinkled on top.

Salads

Steps...

1. Prepare the Dill, either pile all the branches together cutting the very end parts of the large stems with a knife.

Or, take each branch in your hand and snap off the large stem one by one collecting them together with your other hand as shown in the two pictures below and then start chopping thinly.

Finely chopped the dill shown below.

2. Finely chop the Onion

3. Remove most of the white foam that is formed while boiling the Pinto Beans.

4. Its ready when all the water is absorbed as shown in this picture.

Salads

Fresh Herbs Dressing

Serves: N/A

Prep Time: 30 min
Rest Time: 3-4 days

Preparations

1:
Collect all your herbs (either from the garden or freshly bought organic). Wash the herbs while still on their stems and spin them dry. Then Lay them out on a towel to air dry for several hours. (picture 1)

2:
Clean and Dry your hands very well, then remove the stems from the herbs and chop the leaves very finely. For the parsley you can leave the small stems on to make it easier to line up together and chop. For the sage, cut each leaf length wise into thin strips then align and chop. (picture 2)
Do not use a food processor. Doing so will crush the herbs.

3:
Now add all the finely chopped herbs into the big glass jar and mix around with a dry spoon. The herbs will measure to about 1 cup. (picture 3 left)

4:
Fill the Jar with about 4 cups of Olive Oil making sure that all your herbs are covered. If there are any floating herbs, use a spoon to gently knock them down. (picture 3 right)

5:
Next, add 1/2 cup of lemon juice and mix well (you may also add 1-2 tablespoons of apple cider vinegar as an option). Make sure that there is a bit of space between the dressing and the top of the jar (about 1 inch) and cover with a lid. (picture 4)

6:
After allowing the dressing to rest for a few days, mix and taste it. You may add more lemon if you like. To serve, mix well and pour about 2-3 tablespoons (with the herbs) per salad bowl.

Optional:
You can use just olive oil, allowing the herbs to diffuse into the oil for a few days, then mix well and serve. You can mix with lemon or apple cider vinegar to your taste.

Note: This dressing does not need to be refrigerated, and can be kept for around a month to be used on fresh salads or steamed vegetables. Make sure the herbs are submerged in the dressing after serving.

Ingredients

Note: All below herbs are measured after being chopped very finely by hand with a knife (not food processor, to avoid crushing the herbs)

Fresh mint
1 Tablespoon

Fresh Parsley
2 Tablespoons

Fresh Sage
1 teaspoon

Fresh Baby Watercress (optional)
1 Teaspoon

Fresh Rosemary
1 Teaspoon

Fresh Oregano
1-2 Teaspoon

Fresh Lemon thyme
1 Tablespoon

Fresh edible lavender
1/2 Teaspoon

Garlic
2 Cloves (1 Teaspoon crushed)

Red Onion
1 Teaspoon

Fresh Lemon thyme
1 Tablespoon

Lemon Juice
2 Lemons Freshly Squeezed (about 1/2-1 cup, or more If you'd like)

Olive Oil
4-5 Cups

A Big Glass Jar
Measuring 6-7 Cups

Salads

Steps...

1: Collect your herbs: Mint, Parsley, Sage, Rosemary, Oregano, Thyme, and Lavender.

3: Add your freshly chopped herbs (left), 4-5 cups of olive oil, and lemon juice into your jar, leaving about 1 inch of space on the top (right).

2: Chop your herbs and onion very finely with a knife

4: After letting the dressing rest for a few days, stir together with a dry spoon and pour on salads or steamed vegetables.

Salads

Chickpeas with Beets Salad

Serves: 3-4

Prep Time: 45 min
Cook Time: 60 min

Preparations

1:
Soak the dry chickpeas overnight, drain and place in a pot and cover with water by two inches. Add a 1/4 teaspoon salt and bring to rapid boil (quickly scooping away most of the white foam that may form in the first minute). Cover and simmer for about 60 minutes (do not overcook, check halfway through cooking). Drain the chickpeas and leave to cool down before using (see note below).

2:
To cook the beets, peel, wash and cut in halves. Place in a pot and cover with water by about an inch. Bring to rapid boil then cover and simmer for about one hour. Test the beets with a fork, it should go through easily when cooked. Drain and let it cool down before cutting in small cubes. (pic 2)

3:
To prepare the herbs:

Remove and discard the stems from the Mint and chop the leaves finely.

Remove and discard the large stems of the Parsley and Coriander leaving the thin stems only and chop finely.

Remove the tough stem from the Thyme by sliding the leaves between your thumb and index finger from top to bottom against the leaves—then measure one teaspoon.

4:
Dice the Sweet peeper, and onion with a sharp knife (see pic 2, *best not to use food processor for chopping these ingredients*).

5:
Cut the Avocado in half, remove the pit, slice in cubes inside the peel, then scoop out with a spoon.

6:
In a large bowl combine all the ingredients adding lemon juice, salt and olive oil, mix well before serving.

Note: You can serve the water from the boiled chickpeas with some fresh lemon juice while its hot. A light, tasty and soothing soup!

This salad can keep in the fridge for up to 3 days and served cold.

Salads

Ingredients

Dry Chickpeas
1 cup dry chickpeas, which makes 2 cups cooked

Beets
2 small cooked beets, chopped in small cubes

Fresh Parsley
1/4 cup finely chopped fresh Parsley

Fresh Coriander
1/8 cup finely chopped fresh Coriander

Optional: Fresh Thyme
1 teaspoon of fresh or 1/2 teaspoon dry Thyme

Optional: Italian Green Olives
2 large Italian green olives finely diced for more flavour

Red Onion
1/4 cup diced Red Onion

Optional: Red leaf lettuce or baby Romaine
1/2 cup chopped lettuce

Avocado
1 to 2 Avocados cut in small pieces, about 1.5 cups

Cucumber
1/2 cup cut in small pieces

Fresh Mint
1/4 cup finely cut fresh mint

Sweet Pepper
1 small sweet pepper (any colour) or Bell Pepper about 2 tablespoons diced

Lemon
1 fresh lemon juiced

Olive Oil
2-3 tablespoons olive oil

Himalayan Pink Salt
1/4—1/2 teaspoon Himalayan Pink Salt

Steps...

1. Prepare ingredients

2. Finely chop the ingredients with a knife

3. Mix all the ingredients and serve in a large bowl, picture shown without lettuce.

4. Mix all the ingredients and serve in a large bowl, picture shown with lettuce.

Collard Green Salad with Fruit

Serves: 2-3

Prep Time: 20 min
Cook Time: N/A

Preparations

1:
Remove stem from the Collard Greens. Pile the leaves together, roll them and cut into thin strips. See pic 2.

2:
Remove the thick stems from the Basil and Mint and chop them finely. Then measure out with a table spoon.

3:
Take a chunk of pineapple with the core and cut in small cubes, then measure it (picture 1). Cut the apple in small cubes and slice the onions in long thin slices.

4:
Coarsely Crush the nuts with a knife or food processor (picture 3)

5:
Using a small food processor or a coffee grinder, crush the flax seeds into coarse powder.

6:
Place all ingredients in a bowl and mix, let it stand for an hour before serving.

Note: Chopping the ingredients with a knife keeps the texture of the vegetables tasting better than using a food processor.

Crushing fresh flax seeds tastes nicer than using flax seed powder. Do not use flax seed powder from the store.

Ingredients

Collard Green
5 medium Collard Green leaves

Gala Apple
1 small gala apple—about 1/2 cup cubed

Fresh Basil
3 tablespoon fresh basil finely chopped

Fresh Mint
1 tablespoon fresh mint finely chopped

Pineapple
1/2 cup cubed pineapple

Red Onion
1 small red onion

Pecans or Raw Pistachios
1 tablespoon crushed Pecans or Pistachios

Raw Flax Seeds
1 tablespoon crushed flax seeds

Dried Cranberry
1 tablespoon dried cranberry

Fresh Lemon
3 tablespoons of fresh lemon juice

Olive Oil or Flax Seed Oil
1 tablespoon olive or flax seed oil

Himalayan Pink Salt
A pinch (about 1/8 teaspoon) of Himalayan Pink Salt

Steps...

1. Prepare ingredients

2. Remove and discard the stem, pile together, then roll up the leaves and slice thin, then open them up as shown below. The way you cut makes a difference to the taste and texture of the Salad.

3. Crush nuts with a knife

5. Combine all ingredients and leave to stand for an hour, for all the flavours to soak up before serving.

4. Crush flax seeds in a food processor

Salads

Steamed Green Beans & Pine Nuts Salad

Serves: 1-2

Prep Time: 15 min
Cook Time: 10 min

Preparations

1:
Steam the green beans for about 10 minutes. The beans should be tender; the fork should go through and the colour should be sharp green. (Do not over steam).

2:
Cut the garlic in strips and put in a pan with 2 tablespoons of water. Bring to the boil then cover and lower the heat for about 5 minutes until water has evaporated and the garlic is tender. Turn the heat off, letting the garlic cool down in the pan for a few minutes and add the olive oil, pine nuts and a pinch of salt to the garlic and mix.

3:
Place the hot steamed green beans on a plate adding the garlic and pine nuts on top.

4:
Enjoy eating it hot or cold. It can keep in the fridge for up to 4 days.

Ingredients

Fresh Green Beans
2-3 handfuls of fresh Green Beans

Garlic
4 - 5 Fresh Garlic cloves (small to medium)

Pine Nuts
2 tablespoons raw Pine nuts

Olive Oil
1 tablespoon Olive Oil

Himalayan Pink Salt
A pinch of Himalayan Pink Salt about 1/8 teaspoon

Steps...

1. Cut and place garlic in a pan with water

2. Remove from heat and add the pine nuts and olive oil with a pinch of salt

3. Place the beans ontop of the garlic and pine nuts and mix together before serving onto a plate.

Or pour the garlic and pine mix on top of the beans.

Salads

Quinoa and Black Bean Salad

Serves: 3

Prep Time: 20 min *(for the fresh herbs)*
Cook Time: 60 min *(for the beans and the quinoa)*

Preparations

1: To prepare the Quinoa, combine half a cup of dry Quinoa with one cup of water in a pot (the water should cover the quinoa by about 1cm), add 1/4 teaspoon of salt and bring to a rapid boil. Cover and reduce heat and leave to simmer for 1/2 hour until Quinoa is tender but still chewy, and white threads appear around each grain. Take off the heat and leave to cool down before using.

2: Soak 1/2 cup of Black Beans overnight. Drain and place in a pot adding 4 cups of water and bring to rapid boil uncovered. Quickly removing most of the white foam that is formed while boiling for the first minute. Add 1/4 teaspoon of salt, cover and simmer on low heat for 40-50 minutes (check the beans after 30 minutes to make sure its not mushy). Once cooked, drain and leave to cool down.

3: Slice the peppers in long strips, hold together and cut into small pieces.

4: Cut the spring onion into long strips, hold together and chop very small. If the spring onion is too thin then you can cut into small circles right away.

5: Remove the tough stem from the Thyme by sliding the leaves between your thumb and index finger from top to bottom against the leaves—then measure one tablespoon.

6: Remove mint leaves from stem and chop very finely. Measure two tablespoons.

7: Use the very tender part of the Celery heart with its own leaves and chop very finely.

8: Chop one leaf of Kale very finely without the stem (or a whole Baby Kale instead).

9: Mix all above ingredients, adding the lemon juice, salt and hempseed oil before serving.

Note: You can keep in the refrigerator for up to 4 days and should be served cold, never reheated.

Ingredients

Quinoa
1/2 cup dry Quinoa which makes 1 cup cooked

Black Beans
1/2 cup dry black beans, soaked overnight (about 8 hours), which makes 1 cup cooked

Sweet Pepper
1 small sweet pepper (any colour) or Bell Pepper about 2 tablespoons diced

Spring Onion (Scallion)
1 Spring Onion finely chopped

Fresh Thyme
1 tablespoon of fresh Thyme finely chopped

Fresh Mint
1-2 tablespoon of fresh Mint finely chopped

Raw Hulled Hemp Seeds
1-2 tablespoons of raw hulled hemp seeds

Celery leaves
1/3 cup finely chopped Celery leaves, about 4 tablespoons

Baby Kale
1 cup finely chopped baby Kale

Lemon
1/4 cup freshly squeezed Lemon Juice about 3 tablespoons

Hempseeds Oil
2 tablespoons Hempseeds Oil (or Olive Oil)

Himalayan Pink Salt
1/4 teaspoon Himalayan Pink Salt

Steps...

1. Yellow Bell Pepper diced

2. Spring onions finely chopped

3. Finely chop the Celery

4. Remove Thyme from thick stem

5. Discard stems and finely chop the mint leaves

6. Remove and discard the stem from the Kale and chop the leaf as shown.

7. Combine all ingredients and serve

Salads

Red Cabbage Salad

Serves: 2-3

Prep Time: 15 min
Cook Time: N/A

Preparations

1:
Cut the red cabbage in half and shred with the flat side of the shredder (mandolin) (see picture 2). Get rid of the stem after shredding. Alternatively if you don't have a shredder, place the flat side of the half cabbage on a cutting board, and slice thin (same way you would slice an onion) Discard the stem (see picture 2)

2:
Peel and grate the carrots with the other side of the shredder (see picture 3) or use a course cheese grater if you don't have a shredder.

3:
Combine the shredded cabbage and grated carrots with olive oil, lemon juice, salt and pepper, mix well and let it stand at least an hour (or overnight in the fridge) to allow all the flavours to absorb before serving.

4:
This can keep in the fridge for up to 4 days.

Ingredients

Red Cabbage
1/2 Red Cabbage shredded without stem

Carrots
3 medium carrots grated

Lemon
1/2 cup fresh lemon juice

Olive Oil
3-4 tablespoons Olive Oil (about 1/4 of a cup)

Himalayan Pink Salt
1/2 teaspoon Himalayan Pink Salt

Black Pepper
1/4 teaspoon black pepper

Salads

Steps...

1. Ingredients (2 sided mandolin shown, slicing and shredding)

2. Shred the cabbage with a shredder or a knife. Get rid of the stem.

3. Grate the carrots (using shredding side)

4. Let the ingredients soak up for at least an hour before serving

Tabbouleh Salad with Quinoa

Serves: 2-3

Prep Time: 15 min *(for the vegetables)*
Cook Time: 30 min *(for the quinoa)*

Ingredients

Quinoa
1/2 cup dry Quinoa– which makes 1 cup cooked Quinoa

Parsley
2 cups finely chopped Parsley

Spring Onion (Scallions)
1 cup finely chopped spring onion

Tomato
1/2 cup finely chopped tomatoes

Cucumber
1 cup finely chopped cucumber

Lemon
3 tablespoons freshly squeezed lemon juice, about 1/4 cup

Olive Oil
2-3 tablespoons olive oil

Himalayan Pink Salt
1/4 teaspoon Himalayan Pink Salt (for Quinoa)
1/4 teaspoon Himalayan Pink Salt (for the salad)

Preparations

1: To prepare the Quinoa, combine half a cup of dry Quinoa with one cup of water in a pot (the water should cover the quinoa by about 1cm), add 1/4 teaspoon of salt and bring to boil. Cover and reduce heat and leave to simmer for 1/2 hour until Quinoa is tender but still chewy, and white threads appear around each grain. Take off the heat and leave to cool down before using.

2: Pile the Parsley together, cut away the thick part of the stem leaving the upper (thinner) part, then chop finely. Its easier to finely chop if you hold the parsley by its thin stems, bunched together (see picture 2).

3: Remove the bottom root of the spring onion then finely chop. If the spring onion is quite thick, then cut lengthways before chopping (see picture 3).

4: Finely chop the tomatoes and cucumber (see picture 4).

5: Combine all the ingredients adding the Lemon juice, Olive oil and a pinch salt and let it stand for 1-2 hours for the flavours to absorb before serving. Then taste again to see if more salt or lemon is needed to your taste.

Note: This salad can be left in the fridge for 2-3 days. Best to chop ingredients by hand rather than using a food processor for better taste.

Salads

Steps...

1. Ingredients

2. Cut and discard the thick part of the Parsley, pile the rest with its own thin stems and chop (right pic).

3. Spring onions finely chopped

4. Finely chopped

5. Ready to serve

Salads

Broccoli with Flax Seed Dressing

Serves: 2-3

Prep Time: 15 min
Cook Time: 10 min

Preparations

1:
Steam the Broccoli for about 10 minutes, don't over cook. The fork should easily go through the fleurets but not the stem, and the colour still bright green. Place on a plate and allow to cool down.

2:
To prepare the dressing: In a small food processor crush the flax seeds, then add the hazel nuts and continue crushing. Then add the handful of fresh mint on top and crush again.

3:
Place the mix from the food processor in a small bowl and add the olive oil, lemon juice and salt and mix together.
Note: if you add the oil and lemon and continue mixing in the food processor, the dressing will be thicker (like a paste), but will be harder to spread on the fleurets. Use a spoon to scoop out little by little and spread on the fleurets with your fingers (see picture)

4:
Cut the Broccoli in quarters or small pieces after it cools down, then spread the dressing on top. If you prefer you can also use the dressing as a dip with the broccoli.

Ingredients

Broccoli
Broccoli (small heads)

Raw Flax Seed
2 tablespoons flax seeds

Raw Hazel Nuts
3/4 of a cup Hazel nuts

Fresh Mint
1 handful (about 1/2 to 1 cup fresh mint)

Lemon
Half a lemon squeezed (about 2 tablespoons of fresh lemon juice)

Olive Oil
1 tablespoons olive oil

Himalayan Pink Salt
A pinch of Himalayan pink salt (about 1/4 teaspoon)

Steps...

1. Prepare ingredients

2. Top picture is showing the crushed flax seeds.

Bottom picture is showing the crushed flax seeds with the hazel nuts and fresh mint added also.

3. Mix dressing and serve either as a dip or poured on top of the broccoli as shown.

Note: If you add the oil and lemon and continue mixing in the food processor, the dressing will be thicker (like a paste, see left picture), but will be harder to spread on the fleurets. Use a spoon to scoop out little by little and spread on the fleurets with your fingers (see pictures below).

Salads

Zucchini Ravioli

Serves: 2-3

Prep Time: 15 min
Cook Time: N/A

Ingredients

Preparations

1:
Using a knife cut the raw Zucchini in thin circles (see picture 1).

2:
Crush the dry fennel seed and the dry cilantro seeds with a stone grinder until powdery (see picture 2).

3:
In a food processor, place the pumpkin seeds, green fennel leaves (or basil leaves), diced garlic, olives and the crushed seeds and mix for about 10 seconds to make into a paste. Scoop out into a bowl and add half of the lemon juice and olive oil.

4:
Spread this paste between two slices of zucchini and spread a little more on top (as shown below) or you can top it just with the crushed seeds. Drizzle on the remaining lemon juice and olive oil before serving.

Note:

You can eat this right away or keep in the fridge for up to two days. You can prepare this dish with raw butternut squash or beets to substitute for the zucchini.

Zucchini
1 Medium Raw Zucchini cut in thin circles

Raw Pumpkin Seeds
2 tablespoons pumpkin seeds

Fennel Leaves or Basil
1 tablespoon of fresh green fennel leaves (or fresh Basil)

Dry Fennel Seeds
1 teaspoon dry fennel seeds

Dry Cilantro Seeds
1 teaspoon dry cilantro seeds

Lemon Juice
Juice of 1 Fresh Lemon (about 2-3 tablespoons fresh lemon juice)

Italian Green Olives
1-2 Italian green olives cut in small pieces (about 1 tablespoon)

Olive Oil
1 Tablespoon olive oil

Garlic
1 medium garlic clove diced

Steps...

1. Prepare ingredients. (Note the fennel leaves on left side of the board, under the pumpkin seeds)

2. Crush the dry fennel and cilantro seeds with a stone grinder, until powdery.

3. Spread the paste between and on top of the Zucchini as shown.

Salads

Steamed Cauliflower with Basil Dressing

Serves: 2-3

Prep Time: 15 min
Cook Time: 10 min

Preparations

1:
To prepare the dressing: remove and discard the thick stems from the Basil leaves, leaving the thin ones. Combine the Basil leaves, Pine nuts, Pumpkin seeds and crushed garlic into a food processor. Blend for about 25 seconds and then scoop out on a plate. Now add the fresh lemon juice, olive oil, and salt and mix together with a spoon to make a paste.

2:
To prepare the Cauliflower, wash the head of the Cauliflower, cut in half and steam for about 10-15 minutes. Do not over steam. When you can stick a fork easily through the fleurettes, it is ready. Place the cauliflower onto a plate to cool, then cut into separate fleurets. If you prefer you can cut the cauliflower into separate fleurets before steaming if it is easier for you.

3:
Wash your hands and dry them well. Scoop the basil paste with a spoon and use your finger to spread individually on top of each fleurette.

Note: This measure of dressing makes 1/2 a cup of paste, if you want more you can double the amounts.
If you use this dressing for the lettuce & pear salad, add another 2 tablespoons of fresh lemon juice to make it thinner.

Ingredients

Cauliflower
1 large Cauliflower

Fresh Basil
3-4 fluffy cups of fresh Basil leaves

Raw Pine Nuts
2 tablespoons Pine nuts

Raw Pumpkin Seeds
2 tablespoons Pumpkin Seeds

Garlic
1 Garlic Clove, about 1 teaspoon crushed

Lemon
2 tablespoons fresh lemon juice

Olive Oil
1 Tablespoon olive oil

Himalayan Pink Salt
A pinch of Himalayan Pink Salt (about 1/8 teaspoon)

Salads

Steps...

1. Prepare ingredients. (crushed garlic shown on top, and basil with big stems removed and measuring a fluffy cup)

2. Combine basil, pine nuts, pumpkin seeds, and crushed garlic in a food processor.

Mix for 25 seconds.

3. Scoop the paste into a bowl and add the fresh lemon juice, olive oil and salt.

4. Scoop the paste with a spoon then use your finger to push the paste off the spoon and spread on the steamed and cut cauliflower.

Salads

Lettuce & Pear Salad with Basil Dressing

Serves: 2-3

Prep Time: 20 min
Cook Time: N/A

Preparations

1:
To prepare the dressing: remove and discard the thick stems from the Basil leaves, leaving the thin ones. Combine the Basil leaves, Pine nuts, Pumpkin seeds and diced garlic into a food processor. Blend for about 25 seconds and then scoop out on a plate. Now add the fresh lemon juice, olive oil, and salt and mix together with a spoon to make a paste.

2:
Prepare all the ingredients for the salad as shown in picture 3. Then mix all in a bowl along with a pinch of salt, then half of the dressing on top and mix. Garnish with extra pieces of onion and pine-nuts, then top it with the rest of the dressing.

Note: This salad can be kept in the fridge for up to two days.

Ingredients

The Salad

Romaine Lettuce
5 cups Romaine Lettuce chopped small

Cucumber
1 cup Cucumber chopped in small cubes

Pear
1 small Pear chopped in small cubes

Red Onion
1 small red onion thinly sliced (about 1/2 a cup)

Sweet Pepper
2 tablespoons diced Sweet pepper (any colour)

Raw Pine Nuts
1-2 tablespoons Pine nuts

Raw Pumpkin seeds
1-2 tablespoons Pumpkin seeds

Dried Cranberry (Optional)
1 tablespoon dried Cranberry

Italian Green Olive
1 large Italian Green Olive cut into tiny pieces

The Dressing

Fresh Basil
3-4 fluffy cups of fresh Basil leaves

Raw Pine Nuts
2 tablespoons Pine nuts

Raw Pumpkin Seeds
2 tablespoons Pumpkin Seeds

Garlic
1 Garlic Clove, about 1 teaspoon diced

Lemon
4 tablespoons fresh lemon juice

Olive Oil
1 Tablespoon olive oil

Steps...

1. Prepare dressing ingredients and place in a food processor for about 25 seconds.

2. Scoop the paste in a bowl and add in olive oil and lemon juice then mix.

3. Prepare all the ingredients for the Salad as shown. (Lettuce, pear and cucumber cut in small pieces, onion thinly sliced, olives and peppers diced.

4. Mix in the salad ingredients in a bowl and add in half of the Basil dressing. Garnish with extra onion, cranberry, and pine-nuts, then add in the rest of the dressing

Salads

Savoy Cabbage Salad

Serves: 4-5

Prep Time: 25 min
Cook Time: N/A

Preparations

1:
Wash the cabbage whole and dry with a towel squeezing all the water out before cutting in half. Use a mandolin to shred as shown in picture 2 (bottom), or lay the flat side down on a chopping board and slice very thin as shown in picture 2(top).

2:
Peel and grate the carrots with the other side of the shredder (see picture 3) or use a course cheese grater if you don't have a shredder.

3:
Slice the celery lengthwise using a mandolin or knife and then cut the slices into 1 inch long pieces. (see picture 4)

4:
Wash and dry the apple. Then with the skin on, cut into quarters and remove the pits. Then use the other side of the shredder (mandolin) to shred into thin sticks. (see picture 4). If you prefer to use a knife, slice the apple very thinly then cut into sticks.

5:
Cut the onion in half and remove the peel. Lay the flat side down on a chopping board and slice very thinly with a knife. (see picture 3 bottom)

Coarsely crush the Walnuts with a knife or in a food processor giving it a few pulses. Do not over crush the walnuts.

Using a knife finely chop the parsley and mint, then measure them with a tablespoon.

6:
Mix all the ingredients adding the lemon juice, olive oil and salt. You can top with extra crushed walnuts to garnish before serving.

Note: Let the salad sit for a few hours or overnight in the fridge to let the juices soak into the salad. By then, you might need to add extra lemon or salt to taste.
This salad can be kept up to three days in the fridge.

Ingredients

Savoy Cabbage
1/2 a Cabbage head or about 4 cups shredded

Carrot
1 medium carrot (about 1 cup shredded)

Red Onion
1 small red onion (about 1/2 a cup thinly shredded)

Celery
1 stalk of celery, about 1/2 cup thinly sliced and cut to one inch long pieces

Organic Granny Smith Apple
1 Organic Granny Smith apple with peel(about 1/2 cup cut into very thin strips)

Fresh Parsley
1 handful of parsley (about 3-4 tablespoons finely chopped)

Fresh Mint
2 tablespoons finely chopped fresh mint

Walnuts
1/4 cup crushed walnuts

Lemon
1/2 cup freshly squeezed lemon juice

Olive Oil
3-4 tablespoons olive oil

Himalayan Pink Salt
A pinch of Himalayan Pink salt (about 1/4 teaspoon)

Steps...

1. Prepare ingredients

2. Cut or Shred the cabbage.

3. Shred or grate the carrots and slice the onions.

4. Chopped and shredded ingredients ready to mix.

Kohlrabi & Cucumber Salad

Serves: 3-4

Prep Time: 15 min
Cook Time: N/A

Ingredients

Kohlrabi leaves
2 cups chopped very small fresh Kohlrabi leaves

Kohlrabi
1 shredded Kohlrabi (peeled)

Cucumber
2 cucumbers chopped (two cups)

Fresh Parsley
1 large bunch fresh parsley finely chopped

Fresh Mint
1 large bunch fresh mint finely chopped

Fresh Thyme
1 small bunch fresh thyme finely chopped

Fresh Oregano
1 small bunch fresh oregano finely chopped

Fresh Sage
1 small bunch fresh sage finely chopped

Fresh Rosemary
1 small bunch fresh rosemary finely chopped

Fresh Dill
1 small bunch fresh dill finely chopped

Red Onion
1 small red onion (1/2 cup) chopped

Olive Oil
2 tablespoons olive oil

Lemon Juice
1 fresh lemon juice

Himalayan Pink Salt
1/4 teaspoon Himalayan pink salt

Preparations

1:
To prepare the Kohlrabi, see steps pictures in the next page.

2:
Get rid of the harsh or big stems of the herbs and chop them very finely.

3:
Place all ingredients in a bowl adding the lemon, salt and olive oil and mix together before serving.

Salads

Steps... 1/3

1. Prepare the Kohlrabi, it comes in white or red colour.

2. Take stem out, discard and use the leaves. Cut the ends and peel the Kohlrabi.

3. Finely chop the Kohlrabi leaves and shred the Kohlrabi as shown.

Salads

Steps... 2/3

4. Prepare the following herbs: Parsley, Mint, Thyme, Oregano, Sage, Rosemary, Dill.

5. Ingredients prepared and ready to chop (see next page).

Steps... 3/3

6.

Prepare all ingredients (top picture).

Mix together in a large bowl and serve (left picture)

Soups

Black Eye Peas Soup

Serves: 2

Prep Time: 10 min
Cook Time: 40 min

Ingredients

Dry Black Eye Peas
1/2 cup dry black eye peas (soaked for 5 hours)

Fresh Parsley
2 tablespoon (or less) fresh Parsley finely chopped, added to serve

Fresh Mint
2 tablespoon (or less) fresh Mint finely chopped or 1 teaspoon dry Mint, added to serve

Lemon
freshly squeezed lemon juice added to serve

Himalayan Pink Salt
A pinch of Himalayan Pink Salt, about 1/4 teaspoon.

Preparations

1:
Soak the black eye peas for about 5 hours, then drain and place in a pot with 4 cups fresh water, bring to rapid boil, quickly removing most of the foam that is formed for the first 1-2 minutes (see picture).

Then add the salt and cover, leaving to simmer for 20-30 minutes. Check the beans (after 20 minutes, not before) to make sure they are not too mushy.

3:
Serve the soup in a bowl adding 2 tablespoons of freshly chopped Parsley, Mint and lemon juice (to taste) just before serving.

Note: Leaving the pot uncovered for a long time (i.e. more than 1-2 minutes) while removing the foam will prevent the beans from getting soft while cooking.

Soups

Steps...

1. As shown while boiling (left picture), quickly remove most of the foam that is formed for the first 1-2 minutes. Don't worry if some small amounts of foam remains (see right picture).

2. Serve with some freshly chopped Parsley & Mint, adding some fresh lemon juice to taste.

Butternut Squash Soup

Serves: 3-4

Prep Time: 20 min
Cook Time: 60 min

Ingredients

Butternut Squash
1 medium butternut squash (4-5 cups cut in cubes)

Tomatoes
2 medium tomatoes (2 cups chopped)

Onion
1 medium yellow onion (1 cup finely chopped)

Lemon
1 fresh lemon—juiced

Tomato Paste
1 tablespoon tomato paste

Turmeric powder
1/4 teaspoon turmeric powder

Raisins
1-2 tablespoons dried raisins. *(**Hint:** If you prefer not to use raisins, then 1/2 a cup chopped carrots or sweet potatoes may be used instead to sweeten the dish)*

Olive Oil or Sunflower oil
2 tablespoons olive oil or sunflower oil

Black Pepper
A pinch of black pepper about 1/8 teaspoon

Himalayan Pink Salt
1/2 teaspoon Himalayan Pink Salt

Preparations

1:
Peel the butternut squash with a vegetable peeler and remove the seeds, then cut into small cubes (see picture 1).

2:
To prepare the sauce, combine the chopped onion, chopped tomato, turmeric, salt, black pepper, tomato paste and about 1/2 cup of water (see picture 3). Bring to rapid boil on high heat then cover and reduce the heat for about 5-10 minutes. Uncover (leaving on low heat) and mash the ingredients in the pot with the back of the spoon.

3:
Add 4 cups of water, the butternut squash, raisins, and olive oil, leave the pot uncovered and bring to the boil on high heat for about 5-8 minutes.

4:
Cover the pot and lower the heat to medium and leave for about 20 minutes.

5:
Add the lemon juice and bring to the boil, cover the pot and cook for another 20 minutes on low heat. Now ready to serve (see picture 4 for the right consistency). If the soup is too watery, you can leave the pot open while boiling for a few minutes longer to make it thicker. Or you can add more boiling water if the soup is too thick.

Steps...

1. Peel butternut squash and remove seeds, then chop into small chunk cubes.

2. Chop the tomatoes and onions.

3. Making the sauce, left pic before and right pic after mashing into a paste.

4. Combine remaining ingredients as per instructions and cook.

5. Picture shown, ready to serve

Soups

Great Northern Bean Soup

Serves: 5-6

Prep Time: 25 min
Cook Time: 130 min

Ingredients

Preparations

1: In a large pot add the freshly chopped tomatoes, leeks, tomato paste, turmeric, salt and pepper and a 1/4 cup of water, bring to the boil and cover on high heat for 5 minutes. Open the pot and mash the mixture with the back of a spoon then cover for another few minutes and mash again, by now it would be a sauce (see picture 3).

2: Add 8 cups of water, sweet potato, and olive oil (and optional freshly grated ginger) and leave to boil.

3: Meanwhile, drain the (overnight soaked) beans and place in another pot with 6 cups of water and bring to rapid boil, scooping away any white foam that is formed quickly for about 1-2 minutes (see picture 5). In a sink, drain using a colander to get rid of the boiling water, then immediately add the hot beans to the boiling sauce in the first pot. Its important to do this right away while hot, if its cooled before you pour in the hot sauce the beans will remain hard and not cook well.

4: Cover the pot and leave on high heat for about 2 minutes. Then reduce to medium heat for 10 minutes, and then leave on low heat to simmer for about 2 hours until thick.
Now ready to serve by itself or with white or yellow rice (see rice recipes in this book).

Great Northern Beans or White Beans
500 grams (2.5 cups) of dry great northern beans. Soaked overnight (8 hours). Measuring 6 cups after soaking.

Sweet Potato or Yellow/Red Potato
1 Small sweet potato, measuring 1 cup cut in small pieces

Leek or Onion
1 large Leek finely chopped, measuring 1-2 cups *(see picture 2 for cutting method)*. Or 1 medium onion finely chopped measuring about 1 cup

Tomato
3 cups tomatoes chopped into small pieces

Tomato Paste
1 tablespoon tomato paste

Turmeric Powder
1/4 teaspoon turmeric powder

Olive Oil
3 tablespoons olive oil

Himalayan Pink Salt
1/2 teaspoon Himalayan pink salt

Black Pepper
A pinch of black pepper about 1/8 teaspoon

Optional: Fresh Ginger
1/4 teaspoon fresh grated ginger or 1/8 teaspoon dry ginger

Soups

Steps... 1 / 3

1. Dry great northern beans on the left, soaked overnight on the right. Amount in picture shown is for 1 cup dry beans.

2. Cut the leaks lengthways then wash the inside layers, shown at the top below. Cut into thin strips, hold together and dice into small pieces as shown in the bottom part of the picture below.

Soups

Steps... 2 / 3

3. Combine the chopped tomatoes, leeks, turmeric, salt and pepper in a pot on high heat and mash into sauce.

4. Prepare sweet potato to add to mixture in pot

Soups

Steps... 3 / 3

5. Rapidly boil the beans and scoop away any white foam while boiling, then drain in a colander placed in a sink.

6. Immediately add the beans (while still hot) to the sauce mixture and continue to cook them as per instructions. Picture shown ready to serve.

Spinach Soup with Pinto Beans or Chickpeas

Serves: 4-5

Prep Time: 20 min
Cook Time: 40 min

Preparations

1:
In a pot mix the Onion, tomatoes, and 1/2 cup of water and bring to the boil, and mash it with the back of a spoon. Cover for 1-2 min on medium heat then uncover and mash again with the back of a spoon to make a sauce.

2:
Pour in 4 cups of water and add the Spinach, Parsley, Coriander, Dill and the cooked Chickpeas into the pot and bring to the boil while uncovered for 4-5 minutes. **Note:** If you are using the sour dry limes (instead of fresh lemon) you should add it now to the mix, not at the end, as it needs to cook. *(Slightly crack the dry lemons before adding to the mix. Squeeze the dry lemons with the back of a spoon against the pot to release the juices towards the end of the cooking)*

3:
Add the brown rice pasta (making sure covered with 1.5 inch water, if not add more boiling water) and continue to boil for another 2 minutes, then cover the pot and leave to simmer for 30 minutes (until the pasta is soft). **Note:** If you prefer not to use Pasta, you can continue cooking without adding the brown rice pasta, but use only 3 cups water instead of 4 (per step 2 above). May also be served with green, yellow or white rice. *(see rice recipes in this book)*

4:
Now uncover the pot and add the lemon juice (if you are not using the dry sour limes), salt and olive oil. You can add more or less lemon juice to you taste. Serve and enjoy! *(final pic shown cooked with Chickpeas).* **Note:** You can add more boiling water to the soup if the consistency is too thick.

Ingredients

Spinach
4 cups fresh Spinach chopped with the stem or use baby spinach

Parsley
1 cup fresh Parsley chopped

Coriander (Cilantro)
1 cup fresh Coriander chopped with the thin stem

Dill
1 cup fresh Dill chopped with the thin stem

Onion
One small yellow onion (about 1/2 cup chopped)

Fresh Vine Tomatoes
2 vine tomatoes (about 1 cup chopped) or 1 cup tomato sauce from jar

Lemon
The juice of 1 or 2 lemons. Or use 4 dry sour limes (may be found in middle eastern shops, see pictures)

Chickpeas or Pinto Beans
1 cup of cooked Chickpeas, refer to the cooking method in the dry chickpeas recipe in this book. *(Or you can use cooked Pinto Beans or Red Kidney Beans; both can be cooked in the same method as the dry chickpeas)*

Brown Rice Pasta *(Linguini)*
Small bunch (about 20 sticks) of brown rice pasta

Olive Oil
2 tablespoons olive oil

Himalayan Pink Salt
1/4 to 1/2 teaspoon Himalayan pink salt

Black Pepper
Pinch of black pepper (about 1/8 teaspoon)

Soups

Steps...

1. Prepare ingredients. You can use Pinto Beans instead of chickpeas shown. Also you can use fresh tomatoes instead of the tomato sauce shown.

2. Prepare and chop the Spinach. Remove the large bottom of the root (top pic), then pile and coarsely chop the rest as shown (middle pic). Or you can use chopped baby spinach (bottom pic).

3. Cut and discard the thick part of the Parsley, pile the rest with its own thin stems and chop (right pic).

4. Pile the dill (left pic) and chop with its own stem (right pic).

5. Pile and chop the Coriander (Cilantro) with its own thin stems, in the same way as the Parsley, as shown.

6. Final picture show, cooked with Pinto Beans.

Note. Dry sour lime if used instead of fresh lemon. Crack the dry lime with a knife or a fork. As shown.

Lentil and Swiss Chard Soup

Serves: 3-4

Prep Time: 20 min
Cook Time: 100 min

Preparations

1:
In a large pot mix the garlic, Turmeric, Curry, Cumin, Olive Oil, pepper, salt and six cups of water.

2:
Add the chopped Squash, Swiss chard, lentils and Rice (and optional ginger), and bring to the boil on high heat, don't cover, mixing it for about 2-3 minutes. Then lower the heat to medium and cover the pot for 5 minutes. Then lower the heat to low and leave to simmer for about 60-90 minutes.

3:
Check half way through cooking in case more water is needed, if its too thick you can add some boiling water (not too much you don't want it too soupy, you can always add more towards the end if you prefer it more soupy) and continue simmering.

4:
Serve and enjoy!

Note: You can use zucchini instead of yellow squash, also you can use spinach instead of swiss chard or you can do the soup without both vegetables (if doing without vegetables use about 5 cups water instead of 6).

Ingredients

Yellow Squash
2 small yellow squash (about 5 inches long) chopped in small pieces 1/4 inch each piece. (about one cup)

Swiss Chard
4 medium leaves (or 6 large leaves) of Swiss Chard, chopped with the stem (about 1 cup or slightly more)

Red Lentils
1 cup red lentils mixed with 3 tablespoons white rice. Soaked for 0.5 hours and drained

Garlic
4 garlic cloves crushed, about 1 tablespoon

Turmeric Powder
1/2 teaspoon turmeric powder

Curry Powder
1/2 teaspoon curry powder

Cumin Powder
1/2 teaspoon cumin powder

Olive Oil or Sunflower oil
2-3 tablespoons olive oil or Sunflower oil

Black Pepper or Chili powder
Pinch of lack pepper or chili powder about 1/8 teaspoon

Himalayan Pink Salt
1 teaspoon Himalayan pink salt or less to your own taste

Optional: **Fresh Ginger**
1/2 teaspoon ginger powder or 1 teaspoon freshly grounded ginger

Soups

Steps...

1. Chop up and prepare the yellow squash.

2. Chop up and prepare the Swiss Chard.

3. Garlic, turmeric, curry, cumin, olive oil, pepper, salt and water mixed together

4. Adding the squash, Swiss chard, lentils and rice to the mixture.

5. Half way through the cooking all ingredients start to combine. Add more hot water if needed.

(Picture shown is ready to serve)

6. Ready to serve!

Soups

Split Peas Soup

Serves: 3-4

Prep Time: 15 min
Cook Time: 90 min

Ingredients

Green Split Peas
1 cup dry green split peas

Yellow Split Peas
1/2 cup dry yellow split peas

Garlic
3 cloves of garlic (about 1 tablespoon diced)

Red Pepper
1/4 cup diced fresh red pepper

Baby Spinach
2 cups chopped Baby Spinach

Fresh Fennel
1 cup chopped Fennel (with its own tiny green leaves)

Thyme
1/4 teaspoon dry or 1/2 teaspoon fresh Thyme

Turmeric Powder
1/4 teaspoon turmeric powder

Curry Powder
1/4 teaspoon curry powder

Cumin Powder
1/4 teaspoon cumin powder

Olive Oil or Sunflower oil
2-3 tablespoon olive oil or sunflower oil

Himalayan Pink Salt
1/2 teaspoon Himalayan pink salt, or add to your taste

Black Pepper or chili pepper
Pinch of black pepper/chili pepper, about 1/8 teaspoon

Preparations

1:
Mix the Green and Yellow split peas and soak in 3 cups of water overnight (for at least 8 hours), then drain before cooking them.

2:
In a large pot combine all the ingredients (excluding the green and yellow split peas) add one cup of water and bring to rapid boil. Lower the heat to medium and cover halfway for 5 minutes.

3:
Add 40 oz. of water (about 5 cups), add the green and yellow split peas (drained) and bring to rapid boil again while stirring the mixture. Lower the heat and cover, leaving it to simmer for about 90 minutes (or more if you prefer it thicker) before serving.

Note: When the soup is cooled down it tends to be thicker while cold. Whenever you heat again place on low heat, occasionally stirring until steamy and hot before serving.

This soup can store in the fridge for up to 4 days. Or can be frozen (after cooled down) for 2-3 months. When defrosting from freezer leave in the fridge overnight and follow above note for reheating. Or can be placed from the freezer directly in a pot, adding a little water bringing that water to boil and then cover and let defrost and simmer slowly until hot again (occasionally stirring to help defrost).

Soups

Steps...

1. Prepare and chop ingredients. Remember to use the green leaves of the fennel *(top left of the picture below)*, as you can see in the picture below.

2. Combine all ingredients and cook as per instructions.

Picture shown, ready to serve.

Soups

Green Beans Soup

Serves: 3-4

Prep Time: 15 min
Cook Time: 40 min

Preparations

1:
In a large pot place the onions, tomatoes, bell pepper, salt, black pepper and one cup of water and bring to the boil, reduce the heat to medium and cover the pot for 10-15 minutes, then uncover and mash the tomatoes with the back of a spoon. (See Picture 3)

2:
Add 4 cups of water, oil, chopped green beans, potatoes and the carrots to the pot. Increase the heat and bring the mix to the boil, cover the pot half way and let it cook for 5 minutes on high heat. Then lower the heat (medium to low) and cover the pot fully and leave to cook for about 30 minutes.

Note: If you prefer it slightly thicker, to serve with rice as a stew, you can leave on high heat uncovered for 2 minutes.

This can keep refrigerated for up to 5 days, or can be frozen in a container after cooled down to use whenever needed.

To defrost, transfer from freezer into a pot, add a little water (1/4 cup), bring the water to boil then cover on low heat to allow the soup to fully defrost, stirring occasionally to allow it to melt faster and boil again. Or you can leave to defrost in the fridge overnight and then place in a pot, bring to the boil and simmer till its hot.

Ingredients

Fresh Green Beans
2lbs fresh green beans (about 4-5 cups chopped)

Potato
1 medium potato cut in 8 big pieces (or 4-5 baby potatoes cut in halves)

Carrot
1 medium carrot cut in 4 pieces or 4 small carrots

Red Bell Pepper
2 tablespoons diced red pepper

Onion
1 cup chopped onion

Tomatoes
2 cups freshly chopped tomatoes, or 1.5 crushed tomatoes, or 1 cup tomato sauce

Olive Oil or Sunflower Oil
2 tablespoons olive oil or sunflower oil

Black Pepper
Pinch of black pepper about 1/8 teaspoon

Himalayan Pink Salt
1 teaspoon Himalayan pink salt

Soups

Steps...

1. Cut off both tips of the Green Beans, then chop into small pieces.

2. Prepare and chop up all the other ingredients. (You can pre-diced frozen fresh pepper from the freezer as shown below)

3. Mix and Mash the onions, tomatoes & bell pepper and one cup water.

Before Boiling

After 10-15 minutes of boiling. Mashed into a sauce.

4. Add the green beans, carrots and potatoes and cook per instructions. Picture shown below ready to serve.

Stews & Rice Dishes

Okra Stew

Serves: 4

Prep Time: 20 min
Cook Time: 60 min

Ingredients

Okra
3 cups Okra

Yellow Onion
1/2 cup chopped yellow onion

Tomato
2 cups chopped tomatoes

Tomato Paste
1 teaspoon tomato paste

Olive Oil
2 tablespoons olive oil

Fresh Lemon
3 tablespoons fresh lemon juice

Garlic
5 small garlic cloves

Himalayan Pink Salt
1/2 teaspoon Himalayan pink salt

Black Pepper
1/4 teaspoon black pepper

Preparations

1:
Start by washing the okra and trimming away both ends (see picture)

2:
To prepare the sauce, in a large pot place the chopped onion, tomatoes, tomato paste, salt, pepper and 1/2 cup of water on high heat and bring to the boil, cover for 5 minutes. Then uncover and mash the sauce with the back of a spoon.

3:
Add 2 cups of water, the Okra, garlic and olive oil and bring to the boil again on high heat covering the pot half way and leave for 5 minutes.

4:
Lower the heat and add the lemon juice. Cover the pot and leave on medium heat for 25 minutes. Then lower the heat and leave to simmer for a further 30 minutes.

Note: This may be served by itself, or can be enjoyed with cooked rice or rice crackers.

Steps...

1. Trim off both ends of the Okra, and prepare the ingredients.

2. Combine ingredients to prepare the sauce. Before (left side), after cooking and mashing sauce (right side)

3. Add the Okra, garlic and olive oil and cook before adding the lemon juice and leaving to simmer as per instructions.

Stews & Rice Dishes

Dolmma Stew

Serves: 5-6

Prep Time: 30 min
Cook Time: 120 min

Preparations

1: Soak the rice in water for 5 minutes, drain and leave in a bowl. Measure 1/2 cup each of finely chopped: zucchini, beets, onions, carrots, mint, parsley , bell pepper and stems of the Swiss chard. Add all the diced garlic, 1/4 teaspoon salt, 1/4 teaspoon black pepper, 1/4 cup of fresh lemon juice and fresh chili. Mix all this in the bowl with the rice and leave aside to use later.

2: Oil the bottom of the pot with your hand and add a handful of chopped carrots and pepper, then the stems of the swiss chard and carrot strips. (A) , Then Lay out the ingredients in the following order (see pictures): Layer of onion slices at the bottom (B). Zucchini slices on top (C). Two layers of Swiss chard leaves on top (D). Place the rice and vegetables mix on top spreading it evenly (E). Place another layer of zucchini, Swiss chard and onions (F). Followed by whatever you have left of the beets and peppers (G).

3: In a jar mix 1/2 cup of fresh lemon juice, 1/4-1/2 teaspoon salt, 1/2 cup olive oil and 3 cups water and pour over the mixture in the pot. This mixture should roughly fill the pot half way (tilt the pot slightly to see that you have enough, otherwise add a little more water). You can leave this pot in the fridge to stand till next day for cooking or you can cook it right away.

4: To cook, half cover the pot and place on a medium-high heat and bring to the boil. After about 10-15 minutes of boiling you will see the vegetable level go down and notice the water bubbling from in between. Taste the water to make sure it has enough lemon. You don't want to dry out the water completely, so tilt the pot slight to check you still have some water at the bottom. If not you can add some boiling water, but not too much because the vegetables will release more water as they cook. Lower the fire to a low/medium heat, cover all the way, and allow to cook.. After about 10 minutes, check to see that the dolma is semi dry. If not, then leave the pot half covered until it is semi dry.

5: At this point, with the pot fully covered, lower the heat and leave to simmer for at least an hour or two, and then it will be ready to eat. The dish can be left to simmer for longer to make it more tasty. Hint: as mentioned above, as the vegetables cook they release water, so don't add to much water otherwise the dish will come out very mushy. However, if it happens do not worry! It may not look nice but will still taste good!

6: To serve, scoop with a large serving spoon (see picture) and carefully transfer it by sliding it into a large Pyrex dish to keep the layers intact.

Stews & Rice Dishes

Ingredients

Swiss Chard
1 bunch of Swiss Chard. Stems cut into strips and leaves cut in large pieces

White Basmati Rice
1 cup white basmati rice,

Zucchinis
4 medium Zucchinis. Sliced in round circles

Beets
3 Small fresh Beets. Sliced in round circles

Onions
3 medium onions. Sliced in round circles

Carrots
2 medium carrots. Sliced into strips

Mint
1/2 cup finely chopped fresh mint

Parsley
1/2 cup finely chopped fresh parsley

Yellow or Red Bell Pepper
1 yellow or red bell pepper. Sliced in round circles. Remove the stem and seeds.

Garlic
4 garlic cloves. Thinly diced, about 1 tablespoon.

Lemon
3/4 cup fresh lemon juice

Himalayan Pink Salt
3/4 teaspoon Himalayan pink salt

Black Pepper
1/4 teaspoon black pepper

Olive Oil
1/2 cup Olive oil

Chili
1 fresh chilli. (1 Tablespoon chopped finely)
Hint: Wear plastic gloves when handling fresh chilli since the oils can penetrate the skin and remain on skin even after washing hands.

Steps... 1 / 3

1. Cut vegetables to be mixed with the rice.

2. Mix the cut vegetables with the rice.

3. Prepare sliced vegetables for layering in the pot.

4. Prepare Swiss Chard leaves.

Stews & Rice Dishes

Steps... 2 / 3

5. Layer the vegetables in the pot, as per order listed in the instructions.

A.

B.

C.

D.

E.

F.

G.

Stews & Rice Dishes

Steps... 3 / 3

6. After cooking, transfer to a big Pyrex using a large flat serving spoon to scoop from the bottom then transfer by sliding it into the Pyrex dish.

Stews & Rice Dishes

Eggplant Stew *(Tepsi)*

Serves: 5-6

Prep Time: 25 min
Cook Time: 90 min

Ingredients

Eggplant
2 medium sized black/purple skinned eggplants cut in roughly half inch circles

Yellow Onion
2 medium yellow onion, cut into roughly quarter inch thick circles

Tomato
4 medium tomatoes, cut into thin circles

Yellow or Red Pepper
1 yellow or red pepper

Fresh Lemon
2 fresh lemons, juiced, about 1/4 cup

Tomato Sauce
1 cup tomato sauce

Olive Oil
1/4 —1/2 cup olive oil

Himalayan Pink Salt
1/2 teaspoon Himalayan pink salt

Black Pepper
1 pinch of black pepper, sprinkled on top

Optional: Fresh or dry Chili
1 fresh chilli, roughly 1 teaspoon diced, or dry chili powder to taste

Preparations

1:
Oil the base of a large pot with a little olive oil.

2:
Sprinkle at the base of the pot some cubed yellow peppers, finely chopped chili and a layer of onions cut up in circles. (A)

3:
Add a layer of sliced eggplant (B), followed by a layer of sliced tomatoes, and a few circles of yellow/red peppers (C). Add a second layer of eggplant, followed by a second layer of tomatoes and peppers, then top off with any small remaining onion pieces as shown in the pictures (D).

4:
In a small bowl mix the tomato sauce, lemon juice, 1/2 cup water, 1/2 cup olive oil, salt and the chili and pour in the pot. Sprinkling some black pepper on top.

Its best to let this stand for a few hours to let the eggplant release its own water before cooking. This dish can be prepared from the night before, stored overnight in the fridge, and cooked the next day. At this point, when you tilt the pot you will notice the water in between the vegetables.

however if you are pressed for time you can cook immediately. If you choose to cook immediately, start the fire on medium heat and cover the pot to allow the eggplant to release its water for about 1o minutes. At this point you will also notice the water in between the vegetables when you tilt the pot.

5:
To cook, place the pot on a medium/high fire and bring to a boil with the pot partially covered for about 15 minutes. Taste the water to see if more lemon is needed. Once the vegetables are semi dry, cover completely and simmer on a low flame for about half an hour.

6:
At this point the dish is ready to serve and eat. To enhance the flavours you can take the following steps: Using a large flat serving spoon, scoop up the stew from the bottom of the pot and slide into a large flat Pyrex dish. Make sure that the scoops are arranged next to each other and bake (uncovered) in a preheated oven (375F) for 15 minutes before serving, or broil for 5 minutes to dry and make it more crispy.

This dish can be eaten on its own or with white rice.

Steps... 1/3

1. Slice the eggplant into 1/2 inch slices as shown

2. Slice the rest of the vegetables as shown

Stews & Rice Dishes

Steps... 2/3

3. Arrange the layers in the following order as described in the preparations

A.

B.

C.

D.

Stews & Rice Dishes

Steps... 3/3

4. Transfer into a large flat Pyrex dish and bake in oven before serving.

Biryani Veggie Mix

Serves: 3-4

Prep Time: 10 min
Cook Time: 20 min

Preparations

1:
Mix all ingredient in a pot and add 3/4 cup water. Bring to the boil on high heat and keep stirring every minute or so for 8-10 minutes until semi-dry.

2:
Cover and lower the heat leaving to simmer for another 10 minutes until all the water is absorbed. Then uncover and increase the heat and mix a few times until the mixture is completely dry and starts to stick together and to the pot, and starts making a sizzling sound; this is when you will know it is ready.

3:
Uncover and let it cool before storing to make sure water doesn't condense in the pot. If you want a less mushy consistency, use less water when cooking. May be served hot or cold with optional yellow rice. This can keep in the fridge for up to 4 days and may be served cold or hot. To re-heat simmer covered on very low heat until steaming.

Ingredients

Green Peas
2 cups frozen Green Peas

Sweet Potato
2 cups cubed Sweet Potato (or normal Potato if preferred)

Onion
1 small Onion (1 cup diced)

Carrot
1/2 cup Carrot chopped in small pieces

Turmeric Powder
1/2 teaspoon Turmeric powder

Cinnamon
1/2 teaspoon Cinnamon

Cardamom
1/2 teaspoon Cardamom

All Spice
1/4 teaspoon All Spice

Sunflower Oil or Olive Oil
3 tablespoons oil

Himalayan Pink Salt
1/2 teaspoon Himalayan pink salt

Nutmeg
A pinch of Nutmeg (about 1/8 teaspoon) optional

Clove
A pinch of Clove (about 1/8 teaspoon) optional

Stews & Rice Dishes

Steps...

1. Prepare ingredients.

2. Mix all ingredients in a pot with all the spices, oil and water.

3. Heat and mix for 8-10 minutes until most of the water is absorbed.

4. Uncover and continue to heat until mixture sticks together. Mix will have an almost mushy consistency.

5. Ready to serve. Enjoyed hot or cold.

Stews & Rice Dishes

Cauliflower Tepsi

Serves: 4-5

Prep Time: 15 min
Cook Time: 60 min

Preparations

1:
Cut the Cauliflower into flowers and get rid of the hard head that hold the flower together. Cut each individual flower into halves.

2:
Prepare all ingredients as (picture 2). Oil the bottom of a large pot with your hand, then start layering the vegetables on top of each other in the following order: Steps 2/5
A. layer of onions.
B. layer of yam and sweet potato.
C. layer of tomato.
D. layer of carrot, pepper, half of the lemon peel, and half of the garlic.
E. Layer of Cauliflower fleurettes.
F. Layer of remaining tomato, onion, and lemon peel.
G. Parsley on top.
You can also add a few sticks of carrot on the sides of the pot
You can also add a few strips of carrots on the side of the pot.

3:
To prepare the sauce: In a container, mix the lemon juice, salt, tomato paste, olive oil and the spices with 1-1.5 cups of water then pour all over the layered vegetables. (picture 4)

4:
To cook: half cover the pot and place on high-medium heat for 30 minutes until semi-dry, then lower the heat, fully cover the pot and let it to simmer for another 30 minutes until almost dry. At this point the dish is ready to eat.

5:
To serve: Using a big spatula, scoop from the bottom of the pot and slide the Tepsi into a large flat Pyrex arranging the scoops next to each other (See pictures 7 & 8). Add the left over juices on top, and broil in the over uncovered for 5 minutes to crisp up. (Picture 9).

Serve on its own or with rice on the side to enjoy.

Note: Can be kept in the fridge for 4-6 days. Can be eaten cold or heated on low heat covered until steaming again if in a pot, or placed in the oven at 270 if in a Pyrex until steaming again.

Ingredients

Cauliflower
1 Small head of Cauliflower (about 10 flowers after cutting)

Yam or Sweet Potato
1 Small yam or sweet potato cut into circles, or half yam and half sweet potato

Carrot
1 small Carrot cut into circles or sticks

Onion
1 medium onion cut into circles

Sweet Pepper/ Bell Pepper
4 small sweet peppers cut into strips, or 1 medium bell pepper cut into circles

Garlic
3-4 medium garlic cloves sliced in 4-6 pieces each

Lemon Peel
1 tablespoon finely chopped organic lemon peel

Fresh Parsley
1 cup fresh parsley finely chopped

Tomato Paste
1 tablespoon tomato paste

Turmeric Powder
1 teaspoon turmeric powder

Curry Powder
1 teaspoon curry powder

Lemon Juice
1/2 cup fresh lemon juice

Olive Oil
4 tablespoons olive oil

Himalayan Pink Salt
1/2 teaspoon Himalayan pink salt

Nutmeg
1/2 teaspoon Nutmeg powder

Steps... 1/5

1. Ingredients.

2. Prepare and chop ingredients. Lemon peel shown on top cut in small pieces, Carrot on top cut in circles, yam and sweet potato cut in circles in middle. Sliced onion peppers and tomato shown surrounding the sweet potato.

Steps... 2/5

3. Layer the vegetables in the following order as shown

Stews & Rice Dishes

Steps... 3/5

4. Prepare sauce (spices, tomato paste, oil & water).

5. Pour sauce over the vegetables. (Shown before cooking)

6. After cooking

7. Transfer to Pyrex with a big spatula from the bottom of the pot.

8. Slide pieces into Pyrex by pulling the spatula from underneath.

Stews & Rice Dishes

Steps... 4/5

8. Pour the remaining juices on top.

At this point its ready to serve (before broiling).

Stews & Rice Dishes

Steps... 5/5

9. Broil for 5 minutes to crisp up.

Stews & Rice Dishes

Lemon Zucchini with Herbs (Nana'iyi)

Serves: 5-6

Prep Time: 25 min
Cook Time: 80 min

Preparations

1: To prepare the Zucchini, trim off the two ends and slice into thin slices (about 1/4 inch thick and 3-5 inches long). Slice the onion, pepper, and tomatoes into circles (about 1/4 inch thick) . Separately chop a handful of onions and peppers into small pieces.

2: To prepare the Parsley, pile together in a bunch and cut off the thick end of the stems. Then finely chop the thinner part of the stems and the leaves. To prepare the Mint, remove the leaves from the stem and finely chop the Mint leaves. To prepare the garlic, cut the cloves into 2-4 pieces (or leave whole of small).

3: Oil the base of a large pot with a little olive oil, then place a handful of chopped onions and peppers (picture **A**). Then layer the ingredients in the following order (as pictured below):
B. Put a layer of circular sliced onion on top.
C. Layer half of the peppers and garlic and sprinkle half of the chopped parsley and mint on top.
D. Layer half of the zucchini on top.
E. Layer half of the tomato on top.
F. Layer the other half the of the zucchini on top, then the other half of the tomato, then the rest of the onions.
G. Sprinkle the rest of the parsley, mint, and garlic on top.

4: In a jar, combine 1.5 cups of water, lemon juice, tomato sauce, salt, pepper and olive oil and mix, then pour on top of all the ingredients that have been laid in the pot.

5: To cook, half cover the pot and bring to the boil on high heat for about 20 minutes. Lower the heat and cover the pot and leave to simmer for about 50-60 minutes. At this point the dish is ready to eat. If it is not dry enough you can leave it uncovered on medium heat for another 5 minutes.

6: Using a large semi flat serving spoon, scoop up the stew from the bottom of the pot and slide into a large flat Pyrex dish making sure to arrange the scoop next to each other (to maintain the layers). Pour whatever is left from the juices on top, then put into a preheated oven (375) uncovered for 5-10 minutes to dry more. Afterwards you can broil the dish for a few minutes to crisp up.

Note: This dish can be enjoyed either on its own or with white rice.

Ingredients

Zucchini
7 small (about 5" long) or 3 big, (about 1.5 lb) cut in slices

Tomato
4 medium tomatoes, sliced in circles

Bell Pepper
Sweet pepper, 5 small cut in circle or strips or 1 big bell pepper (red or yellow) sliced in circles

Onion
2 medium onions (tennis ball sized), sliced in circles

Garlic
6 small garlic cloves cut in half

Parsley
1 cup fresh Parsley, finely chopped

Mint
1 cup fresh Mint, finely chopped

Lemon
1/2 cup fresh lemon juice

Tomato sauce
1/2 cup tomato sauce

Olive Oil
3 tablespoons olive oil

Himalayan Pink Salt
3/4 teaspoon Himalayan pink salt

Black Pepper
Pinch of black pepper (less than 1/4 teaspoon)

Stews & Rice Dishes

Steps... 1/3

1. Prepare ingredients.

2. Slice tomatoes and Zucchinis as shown.

3. Chop Parsley and Mint. Dice Onions and Peppers.

Stews & Rice Dishes

Steps... 2/3

4. Layer the ingredients as per instructions in the following order.

A.

B.

C.

D.

E.

F.

G.

Stews & Rice Dishes

Steps... 3/3

5. Transfer into a Pyrex dish and place in oven for 5 minutes before serving.

Stews & Rice Dishes

Curry Okra Stew

Serves: 4

Prep Time: 20 min
Cook Time: 60 min

Preparations

1:
To prepare the ingredients; Trim the Okra from both sides. Peel and chop the Celery in small pieces. Clean the Leaks, cut in half lengthwise and wash any mud-soiled layers before chopping in small pieces.

2:
In a large pot, combine all ingredients (excluding the Okra) adding a 1/4 cup of water, stir on high heat for a few minutes, then add an additional 1.5 cups of water and the Okra and bring to the boil, then lower to medium heat, cover and leave to simmer for 15 minutes until most of the water is absorbed.

3:
Add 1/4 cup of fresh lemon juice to the pot and lower the heat and let it simmer for 20 minutes before serving.

4:
This may be served with Yellow Rice (see Yellow Rice recipe) as shown in the picture below.

Ingredients

Okra
2 cups fresh Okra

Celery
1 cup Celery chopped into small pieces

Leek
1 cup Leek chopped into small pieces

Garlic
2 medium garlic cloves cut into small pieces

Olive Oil
2 tablespoons olive oil

Fresh Lemon
1/4 cup fresh lemon juice

Turmeric Powder
1/4 teaspoon Turmeric Powder

Curry Powder
1/4 teaspoon Curry Powder

Fresh Curry Leaves
1-2 tablespoons fresh curry leaves finely chopped

Optional: Green Chili Pepper
1 teaspoon green chili pepper finely chopped

Stews & Rice Dishes

Steps... 1/3

1. Trim off both ends of the Okra, and prepare the ingredients.

2. Fresh curry leaves. To be finely chopped.

Stews & Rice Dishes

Steps... 2/3

3. Combine all ingredients excluding the Okra with 1/4 cup of water and sauté for a few minutes.

4. Add the Okra with 1.5 cups water and continue to cook as per instructions.

Steps... 3/3

5. Ready to serve by itself, or with some yellow rice

Green Rice

Serves: 4

Prep Time: 15 min
Cook Time: 40 min

Ingredients

Rice
2 cups Basmati white rice

Green Lima Beans
1 cup frozen green lima beans

Onion
1 small onion (1/2 cup diced)

Fresh Dill
1/2 cup fresh dill finely chopped

Olive Oil
1/4 cup olive oil

Himalayan Pink Salt
1 teaspoon Himalayan pink salt

Preparations

1:
Soak the rice for 15 minutes and drain it.

2:
Pile the dill and remove the big stems, then finely chop the dill as shown (picture 2).

3:
Cut the onion in half, laying the flat side down, and dice. (picture 3).

4:
Combine the frozen lima beans, dill, onion, salt and 1/2 cup of water in a large pot (picture 4) and sauté on high heat for about 5 minutes. Turn over and stir with a spoon from the bottom up every minute or so until most of the water is absorbed. (picture 5).

5:
Add 2 and a quarter to 2.5 cups of water and bring to the boil, then add the soaked drained rice and mix in well. Leaving uncovered on high heat continue to stir the rice from the bottom up every minute or so until all the water is absorbed (about 4-5 minutes). (picture 6).

6:
Cover and lower the heat leaving to simmer for 30 minutes. Then uncover and turn over the rice with a large spoon from the bottom up a few times and fluff the rice; before covering and leaving to simmer for another 5 minutes. (picture 5). At this point it is ready to serve. (picture 6).

Note: Let the pot fully cool down, and dry the lid of the pot, before putting in the fridge for storage. To reheat, add a couple tablespoons of water and put on low heat covered until the rice is steaming again (about 20-30 minutes). Turn over the rice from the bottom up and fluff, then cover and simmer for another 5 minutes.

Stews & Rice Dishes

Steps... 1/3

1. Prepare ingredients.

2. Remove the big stems and chop the dill finely.

3. Cut the onion in half and lay flat side down. Slice thinly lengthwise then dice small as shown.

Stews & Rice Dishes

Steps... 2/3

4. Combine ingredients with 1/2 cup of water.

5. Sauté for about 5 minutes until water is almost dry.

6. Uncovered on high heat until all water is absorbed.

The rice will appear white and moist.

Steps... 3/3

7. Ready after 35 minutes of simmering.

8. Ready to serve.

Stews & Rice Dishes

Yellow Rice

Serves: 5-6

Prep Time: 25 min
Cook Time: 45 min

Ingredients

White Basmati Rice
2 Cups

Frozen Peas
1/4 Cup

Yellow Onion
1/4 Cup finely chopped

Turmeric Powder
1/2 Teaspoon

Vegetable Oil
3 Tablespoon

Himalayan Pink Salt
1 teaspoon Himalayan pink salt

Preparations

1:
Soak the rice for 15 minutes, then drain it

2:
Add peas, onion, salt, turmeric, oil, and 1/4 cup of water to a large pot. Sauté on high heat while uncovered, stirring every once in a while until most of the water has boiled off (about 4-5 minutes).

3:
Add an additional 2 cups of water and bring it to the boil. Then add the drained rice in. Stir every minute or so from the bottom up until semidry (about 4-5 minutes)

4:
Once most of the water has evaporated, cover the pot and reduce to low heat. Allow the rice to simmer for 30 minutes.

5:
Now, fluff the rice up by gently folding it over from the bottom up, then allow to simmer for another 5 minutes. When the rice is done it will be doubled in size

Note: This dish can be kept in the fridge for 5-7 days. To reheat, sprinkle a couple table spoons of water then allow the rice to gently heat up on low heat until steaming. Once it is steaming, fold the rice over and simmer for another 5 minutes. It will taste as fresh as when you first cooked it! This dish goes great with Bamia (Okra), Curry (Okra), Great Northern Beans Soup, or mixed with Biryani Vegetables.

Stews & Rice Dishes

Steps...

1. Bring rice to a boil stirring from the bottom up every so often until semi-dry (4-5 minutes)

2. When the rice is done it will be doubled in size.

Kitchree Rice (Lentil Rice)

Serves: 5-6

Prep Time: 180 min
Cook Time: 45 min

Ingredients

White Basmati Rice
2 Cups

Dry Red Lentils
1 Cup

Tomato Sauce
1 Cup

Onion
1 Onion, finely chopped

Fresh Garlic
4 Cloves, (about 2 table spoon when crushed)

Himalayan Pink Salt
3/4 Tablespoon

Cumin Powder
1 Teaspoon

Turmeric Powder
1/2 Teaspoon

Olive Oil
3-4 Tablespoon

Preparations

1:
Soak the rice for 15 minutes, add red lentils. Mix and continue to soak for another 10 minutes, then drain and leave on the side. (picture 1).

Note: different lentils require different soaking times. Green lentils will require 2-3 hours of soaking. You will know when a lentil in thoroughly soaked if it is easy to crack open with your teeth.

2:
Cut onion in half. Place the flat side face down, slice thinly, then turn in and dice the slices into small pieces.

3:
Combine crushed garlic, onion, tomato sauce, oil, salt, cumin, turmeric, and 1/2 cup of water into a large pot (picture 2). Leave the pot uncovered on high heat and bring to a boil, stirring every minute or so until the mixture is semi dry. (Mixture should not be stuck to the bottom) should take about 5 mins.

4:
Add 3 cups of water and bring to a boil. Then add the drained rice and lentils and leave on high heat uncovered. Turn the rice over from the bottom every minute or so until semi dry. (picture 3).

5:
Cover and place on low heat. Simmer for 30-35 minutes. Then, with a big spoon, turn it over from the bottom up and fluff the rice up with the side of the spoon. Be sure to not push too hard on the spoon, you don't need to mush it. Then continue to simmer for another 5 minutes. At this point the rice will be ready to eat. (picture 4).

Note: Your own tomato sauce can be made by chopping 2-3 medium fresh tomatoes and mixing them with the chopped onion and 1/2 of water, bring it up to a boil, cover, and place on low heat for about 5 minutes. Then mash the tomatoes with the back of a spoon and continue the recipe from step 3.

You can also cook this same recipe without tomato sauce, resulting in a yellow dish. In this case you combine onion, garlic, salt, cumin, turmeric, 3/4 teaspoon oil, and 1/2 water on high for a few minutes, then add 3 cups of water and continue as instructed (steps 4 and 5). Let the pot fully cool down, and dry the lid of the pot, before putting in the fridge for storage. To reheat, put on low heat covered until the rice is steaming again (about 20-30 minutes). Turn over the rice from the bottom up and fluff, then cover and simmer for another 5 minutes.

Steps...

1: Soaked and drained

2: Mix all ingredients (except for rice and lentils) plus half a cup of water. Mix with a spoon (top pic). After five minutes—semi dry (bottom pic).

3: Semi-dry, not sticking to the bottom of the pot. The grains appear moist, puffed and doubled in size.

4: Rice has somewhat mushy consistency. Ready to eat!

Vegetarian Burgers, Dips & Spreads

Black Beans & Kale Burger

Serves: 2-3

Prep Time: 15 min
Cook Time: 17 min

Preparations

1:
Place half a cup of dry brown rice in a pot, and add to it 1 cup of water and a half teaspoon of salt. Bring to a rapid boil, then cover and leave to simmer for 30 minutes. The water will all be absorbed and the rice cooked and ready.

2:
To cook the black beans, soak them overnight (at least 8 hours), drain and place in a pot. Add water to the top to about 2-3 inches above the beans. Bring to a rapid boil. Quickly scoop off any foam that it formed while boiling, then cover and simmer on low heat for 30-40 minutes. Then drain and let cool.

3:
While the rice is simmering, place Kale, Celery, Tarragon, Thyme, Garlic & Salt in a food processor and give it a few turns until finely chopped. Scoop out of the food processor and place in a bowl.

4:
Mash the cooked rice while hot with a spoon (or pulse 1-2 times in a food processor); then add the black beans, finely chopped vegetables and the oil and mix well in a bowl.

5:
Make little burger patties with the palm of your hands. Dip your fingers into a little bowl of water while making the patties to avoid the mixture sticking to your hands, or use cooking gloves.

6:
Place the patties on a non-stick oven tray or non-stick baking paper and bake in a preheated oven at 375F (190C) for 10 minutes. Followed by 7 minutes on the grill until slight golden/brown.
Note: If using an electric oven, cook time might be quicker than above.

7:
Let it cool down before carefully scooping each burger out with a spatula to avoid breaking it.

Ingredients

Brown Rice
1/2 cup dry uncooked brown Rice (1 cup cooked)

Black Beans
3/4 cup dry uncooked black beans (about 1 cup cooked)

Celery Stalks
2 large celery stalks (about 3/4 of a cup chopped)

Kale Leaves
3 Kale leaves (about 3/4 of a cup chopped without the stem)

Tarragon
1 tablespoon fresh Tarragon (or 1 teaspoon dry Tarragon)

Thyme
1 teaspoon fresh Thyme (or 1/2 teaspoon dry Thyme)

Garlic
2 cloves of fresh garlic, about 1/2 teaspoon crushed

Olive Oil or Sunflower oil
1 tablespoons oil

Himalayan Pink Salt
1/4 teaspoon Himalayan pink salt

Steps...

1. Finely chop the Kale, Celery, Tarragon, Thyme, Garlic with the salt in a food processor.

2. Mash the hot rice with the back of a spoon. Then add the black beans, finely chopped vegetables, herbs, and oil and mix. Then form into patties. Place the formed patties on an oven tray as shown below.

3. Bake in a preheated oven as instructed, then grill until golden/brown. Then leave to cool down in the tray before carefully scooping out of the oven tray and serving.

Vegetarian Burgers, Dips & Spreads

Brown Rice Veggie-Burger

Serves: 4-5

Prep Time: 20 min
Cook Time: 30 min

Preparations

1: Place 1/2 cup of dry brown rice in a pot and add 1 cup of water and 1/2 teaspoon of salt. Bring to a rapid boil for a minute, then cover right away and leave to simmer for 30 minutes. The water should all be absorbed and the rice cooked and ready.

2: While the rice is simmering, combine the Almonds, Pine Nuts, Garlic, Red Onion, Parsley, Basil, Walnut oil and (optional) carrot. Place in a food processor and pulse it 3-4 times to run the ingredients into a paste.
Note: do not over pulse it, you want to be able to taste the nut chunks. (see picture 3)

3: Spread the vegetables paste with a fork on top of the semi hot rice, divide into two portions, and place each portion back in the food processor for five pulses (about 20 seconds). Recombine and mix the portions in a bowl after pulsing.

4: Make little burger patties with the palm of your hands. Dip your fingers into a little bowl of water while making the patties to avoid the mixture sticking to your hands, or use cooking gloves.
At this point it is ready to eat. The patties can be eaten warm right after they have been made, or cold later, but do not reheat the patties to preserve the flavors of the raw herbs and nuts. They can be kept in the fridge for up to 4 days. Can be served while warm or cold with some garden sprouts, tomatoes and cucumbers.

Ingredients

Brown Rice
1/2 cup dry uncooked Brown Rice (1 cup cooked)

Raw Almonds
1 cup crushed Almond

Pine Nuts
1/2 cup crushed Pine Nuts

Garlic
3 small garlic cloves—diced

Red Onion
1-2 tablespoons finely diced Red Onions

Parsley (picture 2)
1 handful of fresh parsley largely chopped, about 1/2 cup

Basil (picture 2)
2 handfuls of fresh basil leaves. (2 cups leaves with tender stems)

Walnut or Almond Oil or Olive Oil
2-3 table spoons of either Walnut, Almond or Olive oil

Himalayan Pink Salt
1/2 teaspoon salt

Optional: Carrot
1/2 a carrot largely chopped

Vegetarian Burgers, Dips & Spreads

Steps...

1. Prepare all the ingredients.

2. Crush the nuts separately. Remove stems from basil, and keep leaves. Use the parsley with thin stems, and chop largely.

3. Pulse the herbs, crushed nuts, optional carrot and oil in food processor 3-4 times to make a paste.

4. Pour and spread the paste over the warm rice, and divide into two portions to be put back into the processor for 20 seconds as instructed.

5. Ready to serve.

Vegetarian Burgers, Dips & Spreads

Chickpeas Dip or Burger

Serves: 5-6

Prep Time: 15 min
Cook Time: 70 min

Ingredients

Chickpeas
1 cup dry chickpeas, soaked overnight (at least 8 hours)

Edamame Beans
1 cup frozen organic shelled Edamame Beans. Can also use frozen green lima beans or frozen green fava beans instead

Quinoa
1 cup dry Quinoa

Parsley
2 handfuls fresh Parsley. (About 2 cups largely chopped)

Cilantro
2 handfuls fresh cilantro (about 2 cups largely chopped)

Yellow or Red Bell Pepper
1/2 medium sized yellow or red pepper

Garlic
4 small Cloves Garlic, about one teaspoon crushed

Red Onion
1/2 medium sized Red Onion quartered, about half a cup

Walnut oil or Olive oil
3-4 tablespoons Walnut oil or Olive oil

Turmeric Powder
1/2 teaspoon Turmeric

Curry Powder
1/2 teaspoon Curry powder

Ginger Powder
1/4 teaspoon Ginger powder

Cumin
1/2 to 3/4 teaspoon Cumin

Himalayan Pink Salt
1/2 teaspoon Himalayan pink Salt

Preparations

1:
Soak the chickpeas overnight (8 hours), drain then place in a pot, cover with water 3 inches above the beans and bring to a rapid boil, quickly removing most of the foam that is formed while boiling for about 1 minute (picture 1). Cover the pot right after and leave to simmer on low heat for 1 hour. Then drain and let the chickpeas cool down.

2:
Place the frozen Edamame beans in a cooking pot, cover with water and bring to the boil, then cover the pot and leave to simmer on low heat for 20-30 minutes, then drain and let it cool down.

3:
Place the Quinoa in a pot with about 2 cups of water (so that the water is about a quarter inch or finger width above the level of the Quinoa), and bring to the boil, then cover the pot and leave to simmer on low heat for about 20-30 minutes (until he water is absorbed).

4:
Split the: cooked chickpeas, cooked Edamame beans, Parsley, Cilantro, Yellow Pepper, Garlic, Red onion and all the spices and salt into two portions, placing one portion of each at a time in the food processor and pulse to dice (picture 2). Then add half the quinoa on top of each portion, and pulse for another 10 seconds. Remove the mixture from the food processor and mix with the walnut oil (or olive oil) in a bowl, combining the two portions.

5:
You can serve this raw as a dip (picture 3), or you can form into patties to be eaten raw (placed on wax paper to prevent sticking and chilled in fridge to settle) or to be baked in a preheated oven at 375F for 15 minutes, followed by 10 minutes under the grill until golden brown.

Note: Do not flip while cooking, and let cool a bit in tray before transferring with a spatula. Electric ovens may require less cooking time.

Vegetarian Burgers, Dips & Spreads

Steps...

1. Remove most of the white foam that is formed while boiling the chickpeas for one minutes.

2. Prepare all the ingredients and place in a food processor for about 10 seconds.

3. Mix the mashed ingredients from the food processor in a bowl with the Walnut oil (or olive oil). You can serve this raw as a dip, as shown below.

4. You can make into Patties and bake in a preheated oven for 15 minutes as per instructions to serve as burgers. Raw Patties or Cooked Patties.

Vegetarian Burgers, Dips & Spreads

Quinoa with Fresh Herbs & Raw Nuts Burger

Serves: 5-6

Prep Time: 25 min
Cook Time: 45 min

Preparations

1:
To cook the Quinoa with the herbs, place in a pot, 1 cup of Quinoa with a little less than 2 cups of water (about a finger above the level of Quinoa), 1/4 teaspoon salt, 1/4 teaspoon turmeric, 1/4 teaspoon ginger, 1/2 teaspoon cumin, mashed garlic and the chopped onion and bring to rapid boil on high heat. Cover and reduce the heat and leave to simmer for 30-40 minutes until the Quinoa is tender and water is all absorbed. Mash the Quinoa while still hot with the back of a spoon in the pot.

2:
Peel and steam the sweet potato and butternut squash for about 15-20 minutes (you will know they are ready when a fork can go through easily). Then mash with the back of a fork (picture 2).

3:
While the Quinoa is cooking, try to prepare the fresh herbs and Pecan paste (picture 3). Place the Pecans in a food processor and grind them finely, then add the Parsley, Cilantro, Carrots, 1/4 teaspoon salt, 1/2 teaspoon cumin and 1/4 teaspoon ginger, then give it a few pulses to mix and form a paste. Add the Almond or Walnut oil and pulse it once again to mix together.

Mix this paste with the mash potatoes and butternut squash (picture 4). Then combine this mixture with the mashed Quinoa and mix altogether. (picture 5)

4:
The final mixture will be quite soft to make burger patties. Put some water in a plate and dip your fingers in the water before making each patty to prevent the mixture sticking to your hands, or use cooking gloves. Then place on a wax paper until its cooled down before serving. (picture 6)

5:
Can be eaten cold on its own, or with rice bread wraps with tomatoes, cucumbers and fresh garden sprouts.

Note: Can be kept in the fridge for up to 4 days, or frozen in a container with wax paper between the layers for up to 2 months. To defrost place on a paper towel and leave in fridge overnight, or leave to heat to room temperature. Do not reheat to avoid changing the taste of the raw nuts and herbs.

Ingredients

Quinoa
1 cup dry Quinoa (2 cups cooked)

Sweet Potato
1 small sweet Potato (1 cup when cooked and mashed)

Butternut Squash
1 piece of Butternut Squash, about the same size as the sweet potato used. (1 cup when cooked and mashed)

Yellow onion
1/2 cup finely diced onion

Parsley
1 handful of fresh parsley, about one cup largely chopped

Cilantro
1 handful of fresh cilantro (coriander) about one cup largely chopped

Carrot
1 small carrot (1/2 cup chopped)

Garlic
1 medium garlic clove (1 tablespoon crushed)

Raw Pecans
1 cup raw Pecans

Almond or Walnut oil
2-3 tablespoons Almond or Walnut oil

Ginger
1 tablespoon freshly grated ginger, or half teaspoon dry

Turmeric
1/4 teaspoon turmeric

Cumin
1/2 teaspoon Cumin powder

Himalayan Pink Salt
1/2 teaspoon Himalayan pink Salt

Vegetarian Burgers, Dips & Spreads

Steps... 1/3

1. Prepare ingredients

2. Mashed sweet potato and butternut squash

3. Fresh herbs and raw Pecans paste

Vegetarian Burgers, Dips & Spreads

Steps... 2/3

4. Mix the paste with the mashed potatoes and butternut squash

5. Add the combined mixture onto the warm cooked Quinoa and mix well together.

Vegetarian Burgers, Dips & Spreads

Steps... 3/3

6. Make into small burger patties and serve.

Vegetarian Burgers, Dips & Spreads

Cauliflower Pattie

Serves: 5-6

Prep Time: 25 min
Cook Time: 45 min

Preparations

1:
Combine one cup of Buckwheat with 2 cups of water and a pinch of salt, bring to the boil then cover and leave to simmer for 30 minutes.

2:
Steam the Cauliflower for 10 minutes until tender. Test with a fork, it should go right through. Leave to cool down then mash it in a food processor for a few seconds. This should yield about 2 cups of mashed Cauliflower.

3:
Mix the cooked Buckwheat with the mashed Cauliflower adding the salt and spices. Then add the freshly chopped tomatoes, onion, parsley and oil. Mix well then shape into patties.

4:
You can serve this raw, or place the patties on a non-stick oven tray and bake in a pre-heated oven at 375F for 15 minutes, followed by 3 minutes under the grill until golden.

5:
Let the patties cool down to harden before carefully transferring to a plate to serve.

Ingredients

Cauliflower
1/2 a Cauliflower

Parsley
1 large handful (about 1 cup chopped) Parsley

Tomato
1 cup freshly chopped Tomatoes

Yellow Onion
1 small yellow Onion finely chopped

Buckwheat
2 cups cooked Buckwheat

Curry Powder
1/2 teaspoon curry powder

Turmeric
1 /2 teaspoon Turmeric powder

Vegetable oil or Olive oil
2 tablespoons vegetable oil or Olive oil (if you prefer to serve raw)

Vegetarian Burgers, Dips & Spreads

Steps... 1/3

1. Prepare ingredients. The cooked Buckwheat in the middle.

2. Using a food processor mash the Cauliflower.

3. Mix the cooked Buckwheat and the mashed Cauliflower.

4. Add the remaining ingredients and mix together.

Vegetarian Burgers, Dips & Spreads

Steps... 2/3

5. Shape into patties, can be served raw or baked.

Before baking

After baking

Vegetarian Burgers, Dips & Spreads

Steps... 3/3

6. Ready to serve hot or cold.

Hummus with Herbs Dip

Serves: It varies

Prep Time: 15 min
Cook Time: N/A

Preparations

1: Soak the chickpeas overnight (8 hours), drain then place in a pot, cover with water 3 inches above the beans and bring to rapid boil, quickly removing most of the foam that is formed while boiling for about 1 minute (picture 1). Cover the pot and leave to simmer on low heat for 1 hour. Then drain and let the chickpeas cool down.

2: Crush the sesame seeds in a small food processor or any grinder until powdery. (picture 2)

3: Pick fresh mint leaves and discard their stems. Coarsely chop the parsley and cilantro discarding big stems. Remove the stem and seeds from the pepper, and chop into pieces. (picture 3)

4: Crush the coriander seed until powdery using a stone grinder or pepper grinder.

5: Now add all prepared ingredients into a large food processor and blend for about 10 minutes until smooth (picture 4).

6: Transfer to a bowl and top off with olive oil (picture 5). You can also garnish with fresh parsley and olives or crushed dry mint leaves with olive oil and chickpeas (picture 6).

Note: Can be stored in the fridge for up to 4 days. Cover the hummus ensuring the cover stays dry to keep it fresh.

Ingredients

Chick Peas
1/2 cup dry chickpeas (1 cup cooked and cooled)

Raw Hulled sesame
1/2 Cup crushed very fine

Buckwheat flower
1/4 Cup

Fresh Parsley
1 handful largely chopped, about 1 Cup

Fresh Mint
1 handful, stems removed, about 1 cup leaves

Fresh Cilantro/Coriander
1 handful, largely chopped, about 1 cup

Fresh Lemon Juice
1/4 cup

Raw Sesame Oil
4 Tablespoons

Salt
A pinch, ~ 1/8 teaspoon

Sweet or hot Green Pepper
1 green pepper, cut into quarters (2 tablespoons diced)

Vegetarian Burgers, Dips & Spreads

Steps...

1: Remove most of the white foam that is formed while boiling the chickpeas for one minute.

2: Crush sesame seeds in a small food processor or grinder until powdery.

3: Chop parsley, cilantro and peppers. And grind sesame seeds as shown.

4: Add all ingredients into a large food processor and blend for about 10 minutes until smooth.

5: Transfer to a bowl and top off with olive oil.

6: Garnish with dry mint, olive oil and chickpeas.

Vegetarian Burgers, Dips & Spreads

Chickpeas Sambousak Spread

Serves: 5-6

Prep Time: 25 min
Cook Time: 45 min

Ingredients

Cooked Chickpeas
1 Cup   *(Refer back to Cooking Dry Chickpeas recipe in this section, on how to cook them)*

Onions
3 Cups, Diced

Turmeric Powder
1/2 Teaspoon

Curry Powder
1/2 Teaspoon

Cumin Powder
3/4 Teaspoon

Himalayan Pink Salt
1 teaspoon Himalayan pink salt

Olive Oil
1 Tablespoon

Preparations

1:   Place the diced onions in a pot with very little water (one tablespoon) and a teaspoon of salt. Then place the pot on a high flame for a minute or so while constantly turning the onions over until it starts steaming. Lower the heat and cover the pot for the onions to be cooked with its own water (the onions will release their own water) for about 10-15 minutes. Check afterwards to see that the onions are soft.

2:   Now add in all the spices (turmeric, curry, and cumin) to the onion and mix, cover, and leave to simmer for another 10-20 minutes for the spices to absorb into the onions.

5:   Uncover the pot and turn the mixture over to dry it off, then add one tablespoon of olive oil and mix together (leaving the flame on low) for another few minutes. Taste to make sure it is soft and the salt and spices are sufficient (you can also add in a pinch of chilli). Then turn off the heat and leave it uncovered.

6:   In a food processor place one cup of cooked chickpeas and give it a few quick pulses to crush it, making sure it does not go very mushy or watery.

7:   Scoop the mashed chickpeas on top of the warm onions, and mash together with the back of a spoon. It is now ready to serve!

Note:

- This can be eaten on its own or you can serve with sprouted bread, or as a gluten free alternative you can use brown rice bread or crackers.

- You can store this filling in the fridge for up to 4 days and enjoy cold, straight out of the fridge.

- This filling can be frozen as well. To defrost take it out of the freezer and leave overnight in the fridge. Be sure to wipe the moisture that collects in the container after defrosting, especially the cover. Then leave in the fridge again.

- Do not heat this dish.

Vegetarian Burgers, Dips & Spreads

Steps...

1. Place chopped onion in a pot.

2. Mashed Chickpeas mixed with onion mixture. Ready to eat!

3. Picture shown after the onion is fully cooked and mixed with spices.

4. Serve with gluten free bread or plain rice crackers.

Vegetarian Burgers, Dips & Spreads

Cooking Dry Chickpeas

Serves: 5-6

Prep Time: Overnight
Cook Time: 60 min

Ingredients

Preparations

Dry Chickpeas
1 Cup Dry Chickpeas

Himalayan Pink Salt
Add to taste

Note: This method of cooking dry chickpeas is used throughout the book to cook dry pinto, red kidney, white kidney, and navy beans. Black eyed peas and Black beans may need less time to cook.

1:
Soak the dry chick peas overnight (at least 8 hours) in water, making sure you put enough water for the chick peas to soak up; at least 4 inches of water above the chickpeas, as they double in size after soaking.

2:
Drain the chickpeas and place in a pot. Add new water until the water level is at least 2-3 inches above the chick peas. You can add more water if you want more broth.

3:
On a medium-high flame, uncovered, bring to rapid boil, quickly removing most of the foam that is formed for the first 1-2 minutes (see picture 1).

Note: Leaving the pot uncovered for a long time (i.e. more than 1-2 minutes) while removing the foam will prevent the beans from getting soft while cooking.

4:
Add a pinch of salt to taste.

5:
Taste the broth, then cover the pot all the way and reduce the flame to low and simmer for about 40-50 minutes. Taste the chickpeas after around 30 minutes to quickly check the consistency of the bean. They should be tender but not mushy. Do not leave the pot uncovered for long while it is cooking.

This can be served in different ways:

- You can serve it hot with its broth adding fresh lemon juice, ginger powder, and fresh mint/parsley, all to taste (picture 2).

- You can drain the chick peas and freeze the broth (once cool) to use at a later time. To defrost, put in a pot with some water and place on low to medium heat until boiling again. You can add some fresh ginger when the broth starts boiling, then simmer for around 10 minutes to get the heat of the ginger, which I personally enjoy when I have a cold.

- The drained chickpeas can be kept in the fridge for up to 4 days, and enjoyed cold on its own, added to salads, or mashed into patties or used for spreads– refer to other recipes in this book.

- You can also store the chickpeas with its broth in the fridge for up to 3 days. Be sure to heat very well (boiling) before eating.

You can freeze the chickpeas with its own broth. To defrost, place in a pot with a little bit of water, and leave on low heat until melted completely, then stir and bring to a boil before eating

Steps...

1. Remove any foam that is formed while boiling (Dry kidney beans will make more foam than dry chickpeas).

2. Served with fresh lemon juice, ginger powder, and fresh mint.

Vegetarian Burgers, Dips & Spreads

Fermented Pickles

Fermented Turnip Pickles
- *Im'Chalela*

Serving Size: It varies,
4-5 pieces with some brine

Prep Time: 20 min
Ferment Time: 10-14 days

Ingredients

Turnips
5 small (about half the size of a tennis ball) hard and very fresh, cut in half

Beets
2-3 small red and yellow, cut into quarters

Carrot
2 small carrots, cut into 2 inch pieces

Himalayan Pink Salt
1 + 1/4 teaspoon for every 8 oz. of water

Filtered/Bottled Water
8 Oz. of water with every 1 + 1/4 teaspoon salt

Preparations

1:
Wash and peel the turnips and cut into four pieces (or 2 inch pieces if using bigger turnips). You do not need to peel the turnips if they are small and organic. (picture 1)

2:
Wash and peel the beets and cut them into pieces smaller than the turnips. (picture 1)

3:
Wash and peel carrots, and cut into 2 inch sticks (picture 1). You should have about double the amount of turnips than beets and carrots.
Note: can be made without carrots, using a majority turnips with a couple of beets.

4:
Wash your hands very well, then put all the cut vegetables into a clean dry glass jar, and stuff them very tightly making sure to evenly distribute the three vegetables throughout the jar (picture 2).

5:
In another clean container make a salt water solution. For every 8 oz. of water put about 1 and 1/4 teaspoon of salt. The water should only taste a little salty. If your solution is too salty the pickles will get ruined. If using sea salt, you may need to use less to ensure that the solution is not too salty (about 1 teaspoon)

6:
Now mix well and pour salt water over your vegetables to fill the jar to the top, then cover tightly with a lid. You can tie a piece of cotton cloth on top of the lid to make sure no air will come in (picture 2). Place the jar on a plate in case it leaks through the fermenting process.

7:
Leave to pickle for 10-14 days (warmer weather can speed up the fermentation process) until the colour changes (picture 4). Open cautiously as it may bubble or fizz (these are good signs!). Use a spoon to skim off any and all white debris that may collect on top, then use a thick paper towel to skim off any remaining small white debris (by gently dipping). This white stuff can ruin your pickles! Use a clean paper towel to dry the lid and rim, and use a spoon to make sure the vegetables are under water. (you can check the pickles for any white debris by day 7. If there isn't any, leave until done.)

Note: do not worry if white debris forms, as it will only be the on the top, and the vegetables under the water will be protected. This is why it is important to keep the vegetables under the water. The vegetables should be crunchy;

Place in fridge after opening, and serve with a clean dry spoon. The pickle water from this recipe can be drank and provides many health benefits since it is full of probiotics from the fermenting process.

Note: If done properly, pickles can be kept for a long time (up to a month or two (or even longer) in the fridge). Making unpasteurized home made pickles ensures that they are filled with probiotics, . I like to eat these pickles with or after a heavy meal to help with digestion.

Steps...

1: Cut the vegetables as shown.

2: Tightly pack vegetables into a jar, then fill to the brim with salt water solution. (Shown below before pickling).

3: Leave to pickle for 10-14 days until the colour changes. It is ok if the pickles leak (like the red dot shown below). While fermenting open cautiously as it may bubble. With either a spoon or paper towel, skim off any white debris that may collect on top. This white stuff can ruin your pickles!

Note: After 10 days, 2ater will be clear of any debris, if not skim off as instructed. Vegetables will also be fully submerged. Cover again and put in fridge (without cloth).

4: Serve with a clean dry spoon. The pickle water from this recipe can be drank and provides many health benefits since it is full of probiotics from the pickling process. Optional: a bit of fresh lemon juice can go nicely with it.

Fermented Pickles

Fermented Sweet Potato / Yam

Serving Size: It varies, 4-5 pieces with some brine

Prep Time: 20 min
Ferment Time: 14 days

Ingredients

Sweet Potato
1 Medium sized potato cut in thin circles

Yam
1/2-1 medium yam, cut in circles

Carrot and Parsnip
3 Medium sized, cut into 2 inch long strips

Sweet Pepper
4 different coloured small sweet peppers, or 1 bell pepper, cut into strips

Shallots
4-5 cut in halves

Garlic
4 cloves cut into pieces

Cilantro Seed
1 Tablespoon

Fennel Seed
1 Tablespoon

Fresh Dill (optional)
Couple of sprigs of dill with stem

Fresh Fennel (optional)
1/2 head cut into strips

Preparations

1:
Peel the sweet potato and yam and cut into thin circles. Peel the carrot (or leave skin on if organic) and cut into 2 inch long strips. Peel the Shallots and cut length wise in half, or quarters. Peel the garlic cloves and cut into small pieces. If using smaller garlic cloves you can leave them whole. Clean the peppers from their seeds, and cut into strips. Cut the fresh Fennel head into strips. (picture 1).

2:
Start by adding the Fennel and Cilantro seeds to the bottom of the jar. Then layer the vegetables (carrots, sweet potatoes/yams, garlic, shallots, and dill) over and over again until you reach the top. Only add the dill in the middle layers, and leave the dill as is on its stem. Make sure you pack the vegetables tightly into the jar, and make sure your top layer is sweet potato. (picture 2 left).

3:
To make the brine, in a separate jar, add a full teaspoon of pink salt for every 8 Oz. of water and mix well until dissolved. Add the brine into your jar until it fully covers all the vegetables, then tuck a piece of cabbage or fennel under the rim to hold the vegetables under the brine. (picture 2 middle).

Note: Never use table salt. You can use Celtic sea salt or regular sea salt. If you use these salts you may need a little more than 1 teaspoon; the water should taste only a bit salty.

4:
Put the lid on (picture 2 right), then tightly cover the rim with a piece of cotton cloth. Do not use airtight lid because you want air to escape during the fermentation process. Date and leave the jar on a plate for 14 days (picture 3). If you use an airtight seal you can loosen the cover and tighten again every few days to let out the air. After 14 days, the Fermented Sweet Potato/Yam will be ready to serve. (picture 4).

Note: After a few days you may notice some leakage on the cloth and fizzling noises. These are both signs that the fermentation is working. Do not open, and leave to completion.

To serve, use a clean dry spoon and fork, and lift the cabbage leaf to serve from underneath. Cover again with the cabbage leaf and press to keep submerged before putting back in fridge. Do not put your hands in the jar, that will spoil the pickles.

Steps...

1: Prepare the ingredients (left) and cut the vegetables as shown (right)

2: Add the vegetables in layer by layer, making sure every layer is tightly packed. Fill the jar with brine, making sure the water comes all the way to the top of the vegetables Then top off with a piece of cabbage or fennel to seal the vegetables in, making sure the water level still covers the cabbage with no pieces floating. Then cover tight.

3: Tie a cotton piece of fabric around the rim and lid tightly as shown.

Leave to ferment without opening for 14 days.

If using an airtight lid, then let the air out every few days as instructed.

4: After 2 weeks of fermenting; your Fermented Sweet Potato will be ready to serve.

It will look like it does here in the picture.

Cover and put in fridge. Can be kept for up to two months or longer.

Fermented Pickles

Fermented Savoy Cabbage *(Sauerkraut)*

Serving Size: It varies, 1/4 to 1/2 a cup

Prep Time: 30 min
Ferment Time: 14 days

Ingredients

Small Head of Savoy Cabbage
4 cups, shredded

Green Apple
1 green apple, 2 cups shredded

Carrot
1 cup cut in circles

Red Onion
1 medium red onion, 1 cup shredded

Sweet Pepper
3 small sweet peppers, 1/2 cup cut into strips

Fresh Parsley
1 cup chopped

Fresh Cilantro
1/2 cup chopped

Preparations

1:
Start by preparing all the ingredients. Wash the cabbage whole, cute in half, then with the flat side down cut the cabbage into strips.   Cut the apple in half, remove the pits, cut into thin slices, then into sticks, (or use a shredder). You can leave the skin on if organic.   Wash and cut the carrot into circles. You do not need to peel it if it is organic.   Peel the onion, cut in half, then with the flat side down slice thinly.   Cut the sweet pepper in half, remove the seeds, then cut into strips.   Chop the parsley and cilantro, leaving the stems on if they are thin. (picture 1)

2:
In one large glass bowl, add the cabbage, onion, parsley, cilantro, and one teaspoon of salt. (picture 2 right). In a second large glass bowl mix the apple, carrot, pepper, and 3/4 teaspoon of salt (picture 2 left). Cover both bowls with a plate for at least 8 hours or overnight (picture 3). Wash your hands and squeeze the cabbage mix every couple of hours, or if left overnight squeeze a few times in the morning, to release the juices.

3:
In a quart sized glass jar, layer the vegetables by first adding a handful of the cabbage mix, then adding a handful of the apple mix, pressing the two layers well. Repeat this until you fill the jar very tightly. (picture 4)

4:
Add a bit of salt water (1/4 cup of water +1/4 teaspoon of salt), just to fill the spaces between the vegetable. Push the vegetables gently with the spoon to allow the water to flow down (picture 5), or gently tap the bottom of the jar on your work surface . Do not overfill since the vegetables will release its own water through the first 4-5 days. You can tell that there is enough water if when you press the top layer of vegetable down and the water covers it.

5:
Cover the vegetables tightly with a piece of cabbage to seal the vegetables under the water. Keeping the vegetables fully submerged (picture 6) ensures that your fermented cabbage will not go moldy. Also make sure that you have about 1 inch of space on the top.

6:
Cover the jar finger tight with a lid (picture 7 left), then tie the neck with a cotton fabric (picture 7 right). Leave the jar at room temperature on a plate for 2 weeks, then open slowly to release the pressure. Be sure that all the air is released before opening fully. All the vegetables should be under the water. The vegetables should taste tangy and crunchy and smell like vinegar pickles. To store, cover again and put in the fridge. It can be kept in the fridge for up to two months or more. If you see any white mold on top, just scoop it out, the rest of the vegetables will be protected underneath the water. To serve, use a clean dry spoon to move the covering cabbage off to the side (don't use your hands) and serve the vegetables underneath. When finished, cover the vegetables with the cabbage again and press the vegetables back under the water before putting back in the fridge. (Same serving method as Fermented Red Cabbage recipe, picture 15)

Steps... 1/3

1: Prepare and cut the vegetables as shown.

2: In the first bowl (left hand side picture), combine your cabbage, onion, parsley, cilantro, and one teaspoon of salt.

In the second (right hand side picture), combine your apple, carrot, pepper, and 3/4 teaspoon of salt.

Fermented Pickles

Steps... 2/3

3: Cover both the bowls overnight.

4: After 8 hours, Layer the vegetables in a jar and press after each layer with a handle.

Fermented Pickles

Steps... 3/3

5: Press it down very tightly. Then add salt water to fill the spaces between the vegetable, push with a spoon to let the water go in, or gently bang the bottom of the jar for the water to go down.

6: Leave one inch of space between the vegetables and the lid.

7: Tie the top with a cotton piece of fabric to absorb any leakage, and leave for two weeks at room temperature to ferment.

This is a two piece air tight cover, You can use a regular cover to make releasing the air easier, otherwise you might hear a big pop sounds sometime within the first few days (do not worry if this happens, just open the lid very slowly after the two weeks for the air to escape, leaving the water inside.

Fermented Pickles

Fermented Red Cabbage

Serving Size: It varies, 1/4 to 1/2 a cup

Prep Time: 40 min
Ferment Time: 14 days

Ingredients

Red Cabbage
1 Medium Head

Celeriac/Celery Root
1 Small root (the size of an apple)

Carrots
3-4 Medium

Red Onion
1 Medium sized

Granny-smith Apple
1 Medium sized

Fresh Lemon or Lime juice
1 Cup

Pink Himalayan Sea Salt
2 Tablespoons

Preparations

1:
Wash and cut the cabbage in half. Remove the hard piece and save few of the outer leaves to cover the vegetables at the end. Place the flat side of the cabbage down and shred with a knife.

Peel the celeriac and carrots and slice into thin strips or circles using either a mandolin or a knife.

Cut the onion in half and peel the skin off. Place the flat side down and shred with a knife. Cut the apple in half. Remove the pits then cut into strips. You can leave the skin on if its organic

2:
Combine all the shredded vegetables in a big glass bowl, top it off with the salt and lemon, mix well, then cover with a place and leave at room temperature for 8 hours or overnight.

3:
The next day, wash your hands and squeeze and turn over the cabbage with your hands to release all its juices. Then start putting it into a glass container. Start by putting two handfuls, then press it down with a handle and repeat until you fill the jar.

4:
Add the remaining juice on top and press.
Tip: the juice should just barely cover the top of the vegetables so that when you push down on the top you would see the vegetables fully submerged. As the vegetables ferment they will release more juice and make a sizzling noise from the air escaping. Juice may also leak out during the fermentation, this is a good sign! Do not open for the two weeks.

5:
Tuck a cabbage leaf over the top of the vegetables under the rim of the jar. Make sure the leaf you use is bigger than the jar so that it will hold down the vegetables tightly. Remove any floating pieces of vegetable out with a spoon. It is very important that all the vegetables are under the water level.

6:
Cover the jar finger tight and wrap tightly with a cotton piece of fabric and date it. After two weeks, open the jar slowly (the same way you would open a bottle of soda). You will hear and feel the air releasing; these are signs that you were successful with your fermentation. You might continue seeing bubbles released when you open the lid.

7:
Check the top to make sure there is no mould (very rare), and if you do see any white, scoop out the first layer and get rid of it; the rest should be protected by the water . Once opened, store in the fridge. This pickle can be kept for a long time.
Tip: the taste should be tangy and crunchy and the smell should be like a pickle with vinegar. Remove the cabbage cover with a clean dry fork and serve from beneath. Make sure to cover again with the cabbage leaf and press down to make sure all the pickle is submerged, then put back in the fridge.

Steps... 1/3

1. Ingredients (left), Celeriac—celery root (right)

2: Remove the hard part of the cabbage. Lay flat and slice with a knife.

3: Peel and shred the carrot and celeriac.

4: Shred the onion, and organic apple with skin.

5: Mix in a bowl.

6: Stuff very tight in a jar, pressing down as much as you can.

Fermented Pickles

Steps... 2/3

7. Add the left over juices

8. Cover with a piece of cabbage. Tightly pack the piece of cabbage under the rim to cover all the shredded vegetable, making sure everything is submerged in the water. If not, you can top off with a little bit of brine (salt water).

9. Wash your hands and tuck the piece of cabbage in.

10. Cover and wrap the neck of the jar with a cotton piece of fabric.

Fermented Pickles

Steps... 3/3

11. Hint: the piece of fabric is red from the leaking juices, just make sure to put them on a plate from the first day to catch any drippings and do not move it until it finishes fermenting. Date it and leave at room temperature for two weeks.

12. After two weeks, cover again and put the vegetables in the fridge to be enjoyed whenever you like.

13. Place the cabbage leaf cover to the side and serve.

14. Ready to eat.

15. After serving, place the top piece of cabbage leaf back on top and press again to make sure everything is under the water level. The top leaf is also edible.

16. Again, make sure all the vegetables are under the water level after pressing before you cover and put back into the fridge.

Fermented Pickles

Fermented Chinese Cabbage

Serving Size: It varies, 1/4 to 1/2 a cup

Prep Time: 30 min
Ferment Time: 14 days

Ingredients

Chinese Cabbage
1 head (about 8 inch long) shredded

Organic Cucumber
1 large organic cucumber (about 6 inch long) cut in circles with peel

Carrot
1 large carrot (about 6 inch long) cut in circles

Parsnip
1 parsnip (about 6 inch long) cut in circles

Bell Pepper/Sweet Pepper
1 medium bell pepper or 5 small sweet pepper (any colour) cut in strips

Red Onion
1 large red onion cut in strips

Fresh or Dry Basil
2 Tablespoon chopped fresh basil or 1 tablespoon dry basil

Fresh or Dry Mint
2 Tablespoon chopped fresh mint or 1 tablespoon dry mint

Fresh Lemon Juice
Freshly squeezed lemon juice (about 1/2-1 Cup)

Garlic
6 small garlic cloves sliced

Himalayan Pink Salt
2 tablespoons Himalayan pink salt

Preparations

1: Shred the cabbage using a knife or a shredder (mandolin). Cut the cucumber, carrot and parsnip into thin circles; do not peel the cucumber. Cut the bell pepper in half getting rid of the seed, then cut into thin strips. Peel and slice the garlic and onion into strips. (Picture 2).

2: First, in a large bowl mix the cabbage and onion, and add the salt. Leave for a couple of hours, then squeeze and turn with your (washed and clean) hands to release all its juices. Squeeze and turn again in another couple of hours (Picture 3).
Then, add the other ingredients on top, mix well and cover with a large plate and leave it overnight at room temperature. (transfer to a big Pyrex before leaving it overnight) (Picture 4).

3: Next day, stuff all the ingredients, with your (washed and clean) hands in a glass jar very tight. Use a handle to firmly press down after each layer (Picture 5). Fill the jar tight leaving only one inch space at the top. Add the leftover juice from the bowl (Picture 6), then cover all the ingredients in the jar with a piece of cabbage (tuck them in very well) (Picture 7). Press it down making sure all the vegetables and the piece of cabbage are submerged under water (Picture 8) (look at the pictures on the next page).

Hint: If the vegetables are not covered with their own juice then add some water to cover the vegetables and add an extra pinch of salt on top. Also remove any floating pieces with a spoon before covering (Picture 9).

4: Cover the jar finger tight and tie the neck of the jar with a piece of cotton fabric. Date it and place the jar on a plate, since the first 4 days of fermentation will cause air build up and may leak due to pressure (which is a good sign!). Do not untie the fabric even if its wet, it will dry by itself. (Fermented food does not like to be moved, so set your jar in a place where it can be left unbothered).

Hint: You can use any thin cotton cloth; sometimes I use an old cut clean t-shirt to make sure the fabric is very soft and stretchy which makes it easier to tie. (Picture 10).

5: Open after two weeks, slowly to release the pressure. Be sure that all the air is released before opening fully. All the vegetables should be under the water. The vegetables should taste tangy and crunchy and smell like vinegar pickles. To store, cover again and put in the fridge. It can be kept in the fridge for up to two months or more. If you see any white mold on top, just scoop it out, the rest of the vegetables will be protected underneath the water. To serve, use a clean dry spoon to move the covering cabbage off to the side (don't use your hands) and serve the vegetables underneath. When finished, cover the vegetables with the cabbage again and press the vegetables back under the water before putting back in the fridge. (Same serving method as Fermented Red Cabbage recipe, picture 15)

Fermented Pickles

Steps... 1/3

1. Wash and prepare all the ingredients.

2. Cut and slice all vegetables as shown.

3. Mix the onion and cabbage (left), squeeze and turn with washed hands every couple of hours (about twice) to release the juices (right).

Fermented Pickles

Steps... 2/3

4. Add the other ingredients on top of the squeezed cabbage and onion an mix well (right), then transfer to a Pyrex and cover and leave overnight (left). (do not leave in plastic).

5. Press down tightly with a handle.   **6.** Pour the extra juice on top.   **7.** Use a piece of cabbage leaf to firmly cover.

8. You should see the juice flow to the top when you press. Otherwise add a bit of extra water and a pinch of pink salt on top.

When you let go from pressing you should see the water covering all the vegetables.

Fermented Pickles

Steps... 3/3

9. Gently scoop out any floating vegetable pieces.

10. Close jar and tie the neck with cotton cloth. Make a triangle with the cotton cloth and tie it firmly around the neck of the jar.

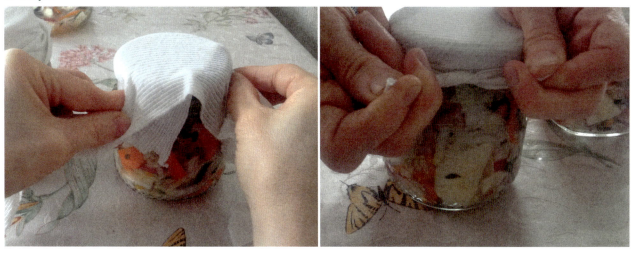

11. Leave on a plate for 2 weeks until ready to serve, after which keep in the fridge as per instructions.

Fermented Pickles

Cucumber Pickles

Serving Size: It varies, about 3 to 4 pieces

Prep Time: 20 min
Ferment Time: 7 days

Ingredients

Pickling Cucumber

Himalayan Pink Salt

Filtered or Bottled Water

Preparations

1:
Use small pickling cucumbers. If they are big you can cut them lengthwise in halves or quarters.

2:
Stuff all the cucumbers in a big glass jar very tightly. Be sure that the jar you use is very clean.

3:
Make a salt water solution in another jar. For every 8 oz. of water add a little bit more than one teaspoon (almost one and a half teaspoons level) of the Himalayan Pink Salt. When you taste the brine is should only taste a bit salty, like the taste when you cook rice. If you use a different salt, the amount needed may vary, but too much or too little will ruin the pickle. Suggestion: taste the water with pink salt so you know the taste to be expected.

4:
Mix well and pour on top of the cucumber jar almost filling it to the top (leaving about a quarter inch space on the top), then cover tightly with the lid and leave until you see the colour change. After about 5-7 days it will turn brownish in colour, then it is ready to eat.

5:
Open the jar. Sometime you will see a bit of white on top. Scoop it out with a spoon and throw it out, or use a thick paper towel to soak up the white water on top and throw it out.

6:
Taste the pickled cucumber, it will have a tangy taste from the probiotics that develop during pickling which is very tasty.

Notes:

- Always use a dry clean spoon or fork to serve the pickles. Do not use your hands.
- Once the pickles are ready, you can put the whole jar in the fridge and it will last for a long time. Just make sure there are no white spots on top!
- Pickles can be kept for around a month. You can also drink a tablespoon or two of the brine at a time if you like.
- If you a see a white bit on the top tip of the cucumber, you can remove that part and keep the rest. The rest of it will be protected under the water.

Steps...

1. Use small pickling cucumbers. If they are big you can cut them lengthwise in halves or quarters. Stuff all the cucumbers in a big glass jar very tightly.

2. Make a salt water solution in another jar. For every 8 oz. of water add almost one and a half (flat) teaspoons of the Himalayan Pink Salt.

3. Mix well and pour on top of the cucumber jar almost filling it to the top, then cover tightly with the lid, date it and leave until you see the colour change. After about 5-7 days it will turn brownish in colour, then it is ready to eat.

4. Open the jar. Sometime you will see a bit of white on top. Scoop it out with a spoon and throw it out, or use a thick paper towel (with a clean hand) to gently soak out the white water on top and remove it.

Note: If you see a white bit on the top tip of the cucumber, you can remove that part and keep the rest. The rest of it will be protected under the water.

Fermented Pickles

For a Sweet Tooth!

Date Sweets *(Medgoga)*

Serves: It varies due to high content of natural sugars

Prep Time: 20 min
Shaping: 20 min

Ingredients

Dates
2 handfuls (about 20 dates or 2 cups)

Raw Walnuts
2 handfuls (about the same amount as the dates, about 2 cups)

Mahlab (Dry Cherry seed)
2 teaspoons grounded
This dried spice can be found in middle eastern shops or some health food stores

Cardamom Powder
1 Teaspoon

Preparations

1:
Remove the pits from all the dates and place in a bowl.

2:
Grind the mahlab until powdery using a mortar and pestle (picture 2) or any grinder.

3:
Put the pitted dates, walnuts, cardamom, and grinded mahlab in a food processor and mix together for a minute or more until it has the consistency shown in the picture 3. Then transfer into a plate.

4:
Start shaping the way you like. It is easiest to shape into a ball by taking a small amount, making a ball with your fingers very gently (picture 4 left), then transferring it between your palms and rolling it (picture 4 right).

Notes: I shape them with my hand, but you can try using cooking gloves to avoid the mixture sticking to your hands until you get the hang of it.

You can also dip the ball in raw coconut flakes and roll around until covered (as shown in picture 6).

This can be stored in the fridge for a long time, and enjoyed as a healthy sweet once in a while. Be sure to keep covered if you store it in the fridge. Wipe the cover after a few hours if you notice moisture. You can place in a container with wax paper between the layers and then cover it. Then place in fridge or freeze it.

Remarks: Keep in mind that dates itself have a high amount of natural sugars. Enjoy once in awhile!

For a Sweet Tooth!

Steps... 1/2

1. Ingredients: you can choose any dates. Majdool dates are one option.

2. Grind mahlab using mortar and pestle until powdery.

3. Combine all ingredients into a food processor then mix to this consistency. Bottom picture is less mixed if you want to feel the crunch of the walnuts.

4. Start shaping the way you like. It is easiest to shape into a ball by taking a small amount, making a ball with your fingers very gently (left), then transferring it between your palms and rolling it (right).

For a Sweet Tooth!

Steps... 2/2

5. These can also be shaped and served differently.

6. Dip in a bowl of raw coconut flakes and roll around until covered. Served dipped in coconut flakes.

For a Sweet Tooth!

Made in the USA
Lexington, KY
03 December 2019